Advance Praise

"Ellen Bremen's book will help students avoid worst-case scenarios in the classroom and on their transcripts, with concrete tools and strategies for communicating effectively with professors. Students will develop skills for college and for life."

–Jennifer Worick, The New York Times bestselling co-author of
The Worst-Case Scenario Survival Handbook: College

"The content is wide-ranging. The voice is conversational and inviting. The advice is specific, clear, and practical—just the sort of information that's likely to help students be more successful in college. I wish I'd known more of this when I was an undergraduate."

–Ron Adler, professor Santa Barbara City College and author of
Understanding Human Communication

"Ellen has amazing wisdom about the inner workings of college. She is the Dear Abby of college professors, such a respectful and open author."

–Vicki Davis, co-founder of Flat Classroom Projects and
author of the award-winning Cool Cat Teacher blog

"*Say This NOT That to Your Professor* gives students the words to say to build a bridge and create the kind of life-changing, student-professor relationships college success is all about. Ellen shows students how to make the most of these relationships to fuel their educational goals. This book is a must-read for every college student."

–Isa Adney, author of
*Community College Success: How to Finish with Friends,
Scholarships, Internships, and the Career of Your Dreams*

"Getting into college is only the beginning. What really counts is squeezing the very most out of your time at college. Ellen Bremen does an excellent job of sharing what it takes to not only survive in college, but more importantly, how to communicate to succeed."

–Lynn O'Shaughnessy
higher-ed expert for CBS MoneyWatch,
consulting director of college planning at
University of California, San Diego Extension,
and author of *The College Solution*, an Amazon best seller

Praise from Ellen's Students and Blog Readers

"Students in Ellen Bremen's class are rewarded with a knowledgeable and truly modern-day professor. She guides her students through the nuances of interpersonal communication, reaching them through her progressive teaching style. Whether teaching her students how to communicate with their professor or how not to express anger, Ellen Bremen inspires learning."

–Spencer Wright

"The information and tools I learned in Ellen Bremen's class, gave me insight into my own thinking and communication style, insight into other styles, and, I believe, helped me become a better communicator. Instead of simply gaining information, her course helped me grow as a person."

–Tisha Gramann

"After Ellen Bremen's class, I felt empowered to step up to the plate and challenge myself. Ellen gives people a voice that is truly amazing!"

–Anthony Endsley

"Ellen Bremen showed me how not just to talk about myself, but how to believe in myself. I am currently empowering myself with an education that will provide me the opportunity of doing what I am capable of instead of just doing what takes the least effort."

–Teresa Covert

"I used your 'I' grade advice today. Thank you! I finished with an A, two B's, and an I."

–Erin Breedlove (student reader from The Chatty Professor blog)

"I feel much better. If I needed to speak with a department chair again, I could without feeling terribly nervous."

–(student reader from The Chatty Professor blog; name withheld)

"I recently asked a professor (early!) what I could do to achieve a 4.0 in his class. He explained his grading system. I turned in my papers early and then made his suggested changes. I aced each assignment. I would not have thought to use Professor Bremen's ideas had I not read her book!"

–Don Crawley, student and author of
The Compassionate Geek: Mastering Customer Service for IT Professionals

Say This, NOT That to Your Professor

36 Talking Tips for College Success

Ellen Bremen, M.A.

NorLightsPress.com
762 State Road 458
Bedford IN 47421

Printed in the United States of America
ISBN: 978-1-935254-68-3

Cover Design: Sammie Justesen
Book Design by Nadene Carter

First printing, 2012

Dedication

I love crazy twists of the universe, and without two brilliant female forces who passed through my universe, this book would not be in your hands:

Sherri Patterson, my beloved best friend for 12 years, registered with me for the Post-Secondary Education program at the University of Nevada, Las Vegas in 1997. We never took one class together.

Sherri was diagnosed with breast cancer, but she encouraged me to continue on. I am who I am as an educator because of that Post-Secondary Ed program. I went into that program because of my Sherri. Sherri died in October 2000, five months after I finished graduate school.

Cheryl Colehour, a new friend in my life since 2010, a fellow mother whose son, August, is buddies with my son, Scott. Cheryl lost her job as an instructional designer and was diagnosed with breast cancer at the same time. While in treatment, she mentioned wanting to do a little work, clamoring for a distraction; I desperately needed an editor for my book proposal, which I just couldn't look at any more.

Cheryl spiritedly took on the job, adeptly capturing my voice and taking my proposal to new levels of elegance and succinctness. When she handed the project back to me, Cheryl simply said, "You know, Ellen, college students *really* need this."

Without Cheryl's masterful touch, I know I wouldn't have landed an agent, or a publisher. Cheryl died in November 2011.

Contents

Section 2: Class Issues Your Professor Won't Discuss With You (And May Not Want You to Know)

Section 1
Class Issues Your Professor Won't Discuss With You(But Wishes Someone Would)

Introduction

Just as you appreciate it **when a professor organizes the material you learn in class**, this introduction is organized with the same structure you'll find throughout the book: **The real story**, then the **back story**. Don't worry, I'll also explain how to use this book before getting into the chapters. But first, here goes: Wonderful student, meet the reason this book is in your hands.

The Real Story

Nicole, a student advisee, sat in my office, firing off complaints about her professor.

> (Quick disclaimer: Throughout this book, you'll read many examples like this one. I'll tell you when the student has a valid point—and when the student doesn't.)

In this case, Nicole was *pissed* because she couldn't follow what was happening in class.

I said, "So what have you told the professor about this?"

Nicole replied, "Nothing. I don't know what to say."

I said, "Well, how can the professor help you if she doesn't know you're struggling?"

Nicole shot back, "I'm just going to fail. I know it."

"Well, you don't have to fail. You could go talk to the prof."

"But I don't get what's going on. She doesn't really care, anyway. If she did, she'd know I'm struggling. It's not like my grades have been *good*."

"Do you want her to come to *you*?" I asked, sincerely, but firmly.

Nicole didn't answer.

"Seriously, Nicole," I said, looking right into her eyes. "What's your role in getting your needs met here? Isn't this *your* education?"

Nicole still didn't say anything.

Just reading our exchange, you may think I was being confrontational, but Nicole and I had an excellent relationship. She'd taken classes with me before, and I knew I could speak to her straight. But my words weren't making an impact.

I realized Nicole just didn't know what to say. I made a mistake by not coaching her with the right words. What's sad is that I knew with every fiber of my being that if Nicole said nothing at all, she could easily slip through the cracks and fail the class—all because she couldn't or wouldn't communicate with that professor.

After our meeting, I started keeping a little list in my desk drawer. A "What Your Professor Wishes You Knew" list. I didn't have any plans for the list. I didn't even know why I was keeping it.

As time passed, I noticed changes in the way students were communicating. I saw students all over campus staring at their phones and texting, rather than engaging in conversation while hanging out or waiting for class to begin.

Then, my own students had *other* issues that required discussion: A late paper, an absence, a failing grade. And I found myself going, "What, what, wha?" in my head over crazy things students would say. Sometimes, I'd want to slap my forehead (that's right, I'd want to slap *myself!*) in frustration because students were doing *nothing* to help their academic issues (remember Nicole?). Instead, they were sabotaging their education when a simple early conversation and a continued connection with me could have salvaged their grade and made them feel a heck of a lot better about their classes and their college experience. Bottom line: Students' communication was changing, and not necessarily for the better.

The bigger problem? Most professors, including myself, won't usually sit the student down and say, "Hey, do you realize you aren't handling this well?" So the disconnect and poor communication continues.

The Back Story

So, now you have it. That's how this book started.

I realized there are tons of college success guides available, but not a single one deals solely with the relationship between the two people who interact in college *every single day*: You and your professor.

Most students don't even think about that when they envision their time in college, right? You're probably worried about how you'll survive Organic Chem and Calculus in one semester, how you'll afford $500 for textbooks, *or* how you'll fit into the campus social scene.

I mean, have you really thought about what *you'll* say when…

…you're going to be absent?

…you turn in a late paper?

…you find a class boring?

…you don't understand why you got a C instead of an A, and you think it's unfair?

Probably not. And you aren't alone. Students who ace classes *and* those who struggle aren't sure what to say either. Then, they pop out the wrong thing.

Professors become frustrated and wonder why students can't speak in a professional, appropriate way. In the meantime, *you're* pissed! You feel misunderstood, and most of all, worried about how this confusion will affect your standing in the class and your grades.

Even worse, your professor may help solve your problem, but rarely, if ever, will she point out your communication errors. Why? A college term has only so many weeks, so we profs see a problem and move to solve it. As I said before, we don't go back and debrief the student on how the communication should have gone down.

Now I know why I started that list: Like I said above, you are going to deal with your professors nearly every day. I'm ready to start talking! I hope you are, too.

College is *the* ideal place for you to practice excellent communication. Professors are among the first people in your life you'll interact with as an adult. And guess what? You don't text with your profs. You don't usually Facebook with them about class issues … even if you Facebook *about* them. You need to deal with most issues face-to-face and sometimes via e-mail.

I want you to have *inside tips* on how to interact so your professors will respond in a positive manner.

I want you to learn what goes on *behind the scenes* of your classes so you can create *opportunities,* rather than fumble over excuses.

I want you to *confidently* and properly stand up for yourself when you're concerned about your classes or grades.

I want you to have improved relationships with your profs, an incredible learning experience, and most of all, *better grades.*

How to Use This Guide

Say This, NOT That to Your Professor is meant to stay with you at all times, either in your backpack or on a digital device. You'll want to have this information accessible so you have the right words to deal with an immediate class-related crisis.

Before you start your classes (or as soon as you have this book), take a quick look at topics in the Table of Contents, such as Absences, Grades, Late Work, etc. When one of these situations hits home (or, better yet, even *before* you have that problem), skip to that section and learn...

The Real Story: Examples of actual students who've faced this situation (whose names and identifying information have been changed for anonymity) and how they handled it—or more likely, mishandled it, and...

The Back Story: A rare glimpse inside a professor's mind. You'll learn what a professor *really* thinks about the way students speak or behave in that situation. Better yet, The Back Story takes you behind the scenes of college policies and class procedures that may hurt you if you don't know how to navigate them. But the right words can empower you, which is exactly what we *want* to happen.

Once you've gained background on your situation, the next sections will move you into positive verbal action.

Ask Yourself This and **Think This, Not That** will help you evaluate current communication patterns and encourage you to change unproductive thoughts you may have about your situation, then...

Say This (the brass ring!) gives you an actual script to practice—or a guide to use and then substitute with your own words—before meeting with your prof to resolve an issue.

The words I'm giving you here are *professional, proactive,* and *effective.* They are the words that a prof *wants* you to say, rather than some of those other, less productive things you *might* say. Use these phrases and you'll earn respect from your professors. You'll have a far greater chance of achieving the outcomes you want. You'll even have early practice dealing with similar issues when you replace your professor's title with that of a supervisor or boss. Isn't that awesome?

Not That shows the ineffective, clueless statements many students use when dealing with a particular class-related problem—things you may be tempted to say yourself.

Are you ready to give yourself an amazing class and college experience?

Are you ready to find your voice? Let's begin the conversation!

P.S. Just so you know, the term *professor* interchangeably refers to pretty much all educators: instructors, facilitators, lecturers, adjuncts, teachers, etc. If someone is teaching you, regardless of their title, the advice I'm offering will probably fit.

P.P.S. Let's get social while you're reading! Jump on Twitter and tweet comments about the book or questions to @ChattyProf with the hashtag #STNT (Say This, NOT That). You can also "Like" The Chatty Professor on Facebook and start dialogue or ask questions there.

Chapter 1

Parents Handling Your Problems

What You May Think:

Mom talked to my teachers in high school when I had problems. I'll let her continue doing her good work.

What Your Professor Thinks:

Your parents may have done high school for you, but they can't (and shouldn't) do college for you.

The Real Story

"My prof writes nasty feedback on my papers. It feels like he's attacking me!"

Beck, one of my advisees, sat in my office, telling me about problems with one of his profs (See? Already, I'm telling you about another student complaining about a prof). He was worried he might not make it through the class, which could affect his graduation plan.

"What does he say?" I asked.

"Things like 'Did you NOT understand this source wasn't credible?'"

Now don't get me wrong, students complain about professors all the time:

We lecture too much.

We grade too hard.

We create tests that contain nothing we covered in class. (Okay, I hated that when I was a student, too).

Students complain about all sorts of things, but Beck's concern seemed valid to me. I wouldn't want someone writing that on my paper either.

"I want to drop his class!" Beck, usually a quiet guy, actually hit a five in volume.

It was mid-term, so Beck would not receive a refund if he withdrew.

And let's be real: We can't always run away from people who upset us, right? We may want to run away (or run over that person with a monster truck), but instead, we have to manage the situation—and ourselves.

"Why not request a meeting with the prof instead? Tell him how his feedback is affecting you," I suggested.

"What would I say?" Beck asked, his face telling me he'd rather have surgery without anesthesia.

"Well, you can say, 'Professor Jones, I appreciate your thoughts about my work, but I'm having trouble with the comments you write on my paper. They seem like you're criticizing me as a person, rather than my writing. I'm starting to get nervous about turning work in. May I have some exact instructions on how to improve?'"

The look on Beck's face told me he was ready to suggest *I* have surgery without anesthesia. He shook his head and his voice lowered again. "I can't do that. I don't like arguments," he muttered.

I said, "Confronting your professor is important so he'll know you aren't comfortable with the way he's teaching you. Think about when you're evaluated by your boss someday. Let's say your boss gets nasty every time he tells you to do something differently. You'd ask the boss for specific feedback because you want to do a good job. This professor may not realize his comments come across in such a demeaning way."

Beck looked doubtful, but picked up his pen and opened his notebook. "So what should I say? Tell me again."

Beck agreed he'd make an appointment with the prof the next day and then let me know what happened.

Well, get ready for a twist ... Beck didn't see the professor.

His mother did.

You heard me right.

But first, Beck's mother called me: "Mrs. Bremen, Beck is having big trouble with one of his professors," she snapped. "This guy is using too much negative reinforcement with my son. He treats Beck like he does nothing right even when he's trying his hardest. I want to schedule a meeting with this jerk and find out why he's putting down my kid!"

"I'm sorry," I said. "Legally, I can't discuss this situation with you."

"What do you mean?" she growled. "That's crazy. This is my kid! I'm paying good money for his education and I have a right to know what's going on."

The Back Story

Are you surprised I used the word *legally?* I'm not a lawyer, nor do I play one on TV or cable, but I do know about The Family Educational Rights and Privacy Act of 1974 (FERPA), a law enabling students to keep their education a private matter once they hit age 18.

So, legally your professors cannot discuss how you're doing with your parents without your permission. The only exception to this law is if you sign paperwork with the Registrar's office giving Mom or Dad freedom to see your educational records or speak to your profs.

Are you having a small party in your head right now? Woo hoo! Dad can't pick up the phone and randomly call your professor for status updates! You're in the clear!

Other students, like Beck, or helicopter parents, like his mother, are shocked by this law. Let's face it: if Mom and Dad have been stomping into his classroom or principal's office every time Beck's pencil broke, taking care of his own college business is going to be a shift for both parties.

Most of the phone calls I receive from parents are well-intentioned. Maybe Jamison's parents are getting divorced, and he's so upset his concentration is threatened. Perhaps Jacqueline is telling her parents she's going to class, but instead she's heading down the street to her 40-year-old boyfriend's house. Maybe Jake's parents have been blindsided by bad report cards when he told them he was doing well.

I'm a mom of two young kids, ages 4 and 9. I imagine it's a gigantic adjustment to go from annual parent-teacher conferences and full access to a child's educational information to no information—other than what my child chooses to tell me—once college starts. I would want to know my hard-earned money, or my son or daughter's scholarship or financial aid, isn't going to waste. I would want to know if my daughter is drooling and snoring in bed rather than sitting in class. I also want to know if she's struggling in a class she *is* attending.

As a professor, I take a different position on this subject.

Without your parents having front-line, hovering knowledge of your educational issues, you're forced to take care of them yourself. I'm not saying you should keep your academic struggles from your parents, but *you* need to start that conversation. Then, you can tell your parents about options you're exploring and get their feedback. They will be impressed and proud of you for working through your own obstacles—even if they get heavy-handed with the advice.

Ask Yourself This:

Did my mom and dad handle school problems for me in high school? If so, did I want them to go talk to my teachers or the principal? When they intervened, did it make me feel angry, untrustworthy, irresponsible, relieved, or thankful?

Did I ever go to teachers on my own for help? What was the best experience I had talking to a teacher when I needed help? What was the worst experience?

If I went to a teacher for help and created a positive outcome, did that make me feel confident, happy, and motivated?

Think This:

If my parents previously handled my school business, taking on these issues will be a switch for me. If I have ever taken on an academic issue by myself, then I have proven to myself that I can handle it.

I realize college feels different. You may be terrified to confront your professors. Totally understandable, but think about it: As long as you stay in control and speak in a calm, professional way, what's the worst that can happen? It's not like you're going to lose your job or get kicked out of school just for standing up for yourself. Your professor isn't going to bite your wrist, and technically she can't drop your grade just because she doesn't like what you have to say. She may be gruff, grumpy, or whatever, but a rough demeanor doesn't translate into you getting a poor grade.

If the conversation doesn't go well, you can go higher—to the department chair, division chair—even the dean of instruction or vice president of the college (See Chapter 31). Colleges have a chain of command, just like any other business. Chances are you'll be able to work out the situation before any of that happens. Believe in yourself.

Use good words to solve the issue. You'll feel more confident every time you try.

Not That:

I'm going to drop this class because I can't stand this professor!

A term is only 10-15 weeks at most (depending on quarter or semester). Even if you can't get through to your professor with the communication tips I recommend, you won't be with this person forever.

And what happens if you don't like the next professor who teaches this subject? Are you going to keep dropping classes and losing money? Stick it out. You'll learn far more by staying with a challenging situation and overcoming it than by running away. Staying in the wolf's den will increase your confidence when other wolves bare their teeth.

I'm going to sign the darned FER-whatever paper so my Mom or Dad can go tell that guy off!

Are you kidding? This is college! You're an adult, remember? It's time to fight your own battles. Having your parents save the day won't give you the practice you need to deal with conflict in the future. What's next? Having Mom defend you during an argument with your best friend? Having Dad sit down for a little chat with your girlfriend when she changes her relationship status on Facebook? Let me give you one more dose of reality: Believe it or not, some students bring parents to job interviews. Seriously. Employers never look upon this favorably and those students do not get jobs. If you can't imagine taking Mom or Dad to a job interview or solving your relationship issues (and hopefully that makes you cringe to even think about), then don't have Mom or Dad do college for you.

Say This:

If you come across a frustrating situation with a professor, similar to the problem Beck experienced, do what he should have done. Make an appointment with the professor and say,

Thank you for taking time to see me today, Professor Frodo. When I read the comments you make on my papers, I feel like you're attacking my work. This is the way I'm taking your words and I could be mistaken, but I have a hard time focusing on improving my work when the comments seem so harsh. Can we talk about what's wrong with my papers so I can improve them?

You can use this same strategy to deal with any other issue where you feel a professor is treating you poorly. This doesn't occur often, but whether perceived or real, it can happen. Sometimes a student will say to me, "That professor just doesn't like me."

I do *not* recommend going to your professor and saying, "I don't think you like me." The professor doesn't have to like you. The professor has to be fair in his instruction and grading. A friendly working relationship is a bonus, and more often than not, it will happen. Instead, you should say to a prof,

> I have a lot to learn from you, but I'm getting a sense you're frustrated with me or my work. I want to do my best in this class. Is there something I need to do differently?

Not That:

> You must not like me very much to say these things.
>
> I must be a total screw up, and I can't do anything right in this class.
>
> You're a real jerk, and you must not care about your students' feelings.

Acting angry or becoming a victim will not get your message across. Instead, ask questions and use "I" language—as sampled in the previous "Say This" example—to focus on what you're thinking and feeling.

The End Note

Are you wondering what happened with Beck?

My last words to Beck's mother were, "If a student comes to me about problems with a professor, I usually suggest he make an appointment and speak directly to that professor."

So she did. Even though I warned her that Professor Jones wouldn't be able to speak to her without the signed FERPA paperwork. Beck's helicopter mother took a city tour of the prof's office: She swooped right in during his next office hour.

Here's where I'm concerned about this situation: Beck missed a huge opportunity to advocate for himself—an experience that could have given him confidence for future conflict situations. And what if he has a different issue with another professor next semester, or the one after that? At what point will he take responsibility for his education—and earn his professor's respect?

Here's another quick story: Mary was a struggling student of mine, all by her own doing. She skipped class, didn't follow through on assignments or studying, and semester after semester, repeatedly fell apart on promises to her parents that she would do better.

Mary did sign the FERPA paperwork giving her parents access to her records and her profs right at the outset of her college career, but it didn't make any difference. The only benefit Mary's parents had was the ability to find out directly from a prof just how poorly Mary was doing—and how much money was wasted on her education. Not surprisingly, Mary ended up on academic probation, which required a hearing.

Ready for another twist? Mary *didn't* have her parents attend the hearing. She went alone. I wasn't expecting her explanation: "If my parents came, I knew I wouldn't take it seriously. I probably needed it to happen and I needed to do it on my own." Mary did turn things around for herself. Her chosen independence at the academic hearing was a clear first step.

Let's focus on how handling your own problems in college can benefit you.

- You'll likely have a better relationship with your professor, especially if your conversation goes well.
- You'll have a better idea of what this person who's grading your work is expecting from you—and that's vital to your success. Having a stronger feedback loop gives you a chance to get better grades because you know what's required.
- You'll gain confidence in dealing with conflicts. If you need to confront another professor, you'll have this experience to draw on.

Speaking of conflict management, let's look at the future for a second. Conflict is all over our everyday lives. You probably know that. Some parents may argue that an 18-year-old is an adult in body, but not necessarily emotionally mature enough to handle stressful confrontations. I say that at 18, high school is over and it's time to start figuring out the rest of the world. You're in college anyway, so why not use the people and situations there as a safe training ground to deal with conflict and practice resolving situations in an assertive, professional, and proactive manner?

Bottom line: College has no PTA. Parents cannot and should not handle college-related problems for you.

Join your own SPA: The Student-Professor Association.
    You hold all the meetings.
    You set the agendas.
    You gain all the academic benefits.
    And they last a lifetime.

Chapter 2

Class Jokers

What You May Think:
Everyone loved my jokes in high school.

What Your Professor Thinks:
Leave your act back in high school. It won't work in college.

The Real Story

Jake and Marshall are two students I'll never forget, because they made their comedic debut on the first day of one of my speech classes—within the first five minutes, to be exact. I always start class by telling students about my background. Before I uttered more than a few sentences, Jake raised his hand and asked, "Are you gay?"

So far, I'd only given them my name and educational background, so I have absolutely no idea where this question came from. I'm rarely speechless, but in that moment I had no words. All I came up with was, "Give me a few more seconds and I'll tell you about my husband and new baby."

To my relief, I only heard a few random giggles. I had an entire class to consider and knew my response would set a precedent. Remember, we weren't even past the first fifteen minutes on the *first* day.

Did the fun stop there? No. I didn't escape so easily. After reviewing the syllabus, I asked the students to form small groups for our introductory activity. Of course, Jake and Marshall stuck together. I walked around the room to make sure everyone was teamed, then I heard laughter in different parts of the room. I looked behind me and there was Marshall lying face-down on one of the long tables. Some students shook their heads in disgust, while others laughed.

I walked over to Marshall, bent down, and cocked my head sideways so I could see him eye-to-eye. I could feel myself starting to fume but tried to steady my words. I said, "Wow, you must be really tired. You do 5 a.m. drills on the soccer team, right?"

"Yeah," he said sleepily. "This morning."

"I'd be toast if I did that," I said. "Um, do you think you could sit in your seat for a bit?"

You're probably thinking I set the precedent of a doormat, but really, getting the kid upright was my main goal at that moment. Fortunately, other than a few distracting comments, Jake and Marshall produced no other major comedic displays. We made it through class. I wanted to talk to the duo once class ended—a private, brief conversation about classroom conduct—but they dashed out the door. Suddenly, I found myself surrounded by five other students.

"Those two are going to be really interesting," one said.

Another student piped up, "I don't know if I can give a speech in front of those guys."

Two other students nodded.

Wonderful. Public Speaking 101 is stressful enough. Now students felt they couldn't speak? I didn't blame them for feeling concerned: If I was targeted, anyone else could be. I assured the students I would handle the situation—quickly.

The next day, Jake and Marshall arrived a few minutes late. I was at the computer in front of my classroom giving an overview of the course management system. When I stepped away from the computer to point to an area of the screen, Jake came up and sat at the computer…

…while I was speaking!

I gave him a stern look and pointed to his seat. I couldn't *believe* I was dealing with a college student!

That day, once we got into our activity, I made my way over to Jake and Marshall and said quietly, "I need to speak with you after class. Please stay."

As I walked around and monitored the other groups, to my surprise, I overheard some other comments:

"They haven't changed since high school."

"Those guys are still idiots."

"They pull this crap in Dr. W's class all the time."

"They've been hit in the head with too many soccer balls."

Jake and Marshall were infecting my class, and it was only day two. Later, I sat down with Jake and Marshall and said, "Hey, guys, I love your energy, but the comments ... the computer... We're early on in the semester and I'm worried. The class is getting disrupted and I've got to tell you, a few students have told me they're too intimidated to give a speech in front of you. Like they might be your next target."

Marshall scrunched his face and raised an eyebrow, "Like we'd really do something to mess up someone else's speech."

"Well, the other students don't know that," I replied. "They can only go by what they've seen these past two days. And, some of them know you from high school, and I hear you were pretty interesting there, too." (I tried to say this in earnest, without any note of sarcasm).

Probably no surprise they actually found *that* comment funny.

Jake and Marshall assured me they wouldn't create a problem. And they didn't. Much.

In class, they still responded to open discussion somewhat inappropriately.

They still engaged in side-talk far more often than they should have.

They were quasi-focused during speeches.

Bottom line? Their behavior continued to create a "mood" for my class. And it wasn't a good mood.

The Back Story

I see this all the time: A class joker whose former one-man (or woman) show ran weekly in high school decides to reinvent the act in a college classroom. In high school, the class joker is the hero, a welcome diversion to get everyone through an otherwise mind-numbing class. Everyone admires his boldness and self-confidence. And let's not forget popularity: In high school, the class joker typically has a wide fan base.

In college, jokers like Jake and Marshall face a different experience. They are no longer hilarious *or* popular. Instead, they're the target of judgmental whispers and after-class conversations among fellow students. Unlike high school, most college students actually *want* to learn and they do not welcome distractions.

For a prof, the class joker is an energy drain and a source of stress. Profs spend long hours preparing for classes and, speaking for myself, I always feel a little anxiety over how class dynamics will play out. A situation like the one I faced with Jake and Marshall threatens the entire class tone. I have to consider my students' reactions and their comfort level. I don't look forward to subsequent classes quite as much because I wonder what that day's behavior will bring. I want my class to be an open, enjoyable place for all students, but when a joker undermines the class, my whole energy is focused on their bad behavior—not on teaching or enjoying my other students and their engagement.

A class can easily derail when influenced by jokers, so it's my job to fix the situation quickly. Of course, that's easier said than done. One method is shaming the offenders, but that's not how I prefer to use my authority. I had two professors like that: A psychology prof who ridiculed late students all hour long (I know ... he taught what?), and a literature prof who locked the door at the top of the hour, forcing students to knock. I swore I would never be that person, although I can't say in this case a bit of embarrassment didn't cross my mind.

I prefer to do exactly what I did with Jake and Marshall: Directly manage the situation by talking to the students privately and trying to help them recognize the inappropriateness of their behavior.

Keep in mind that I do have another option—an official one: Based on the Student Code of Conduct, I could have tossed these students out of class. Some professors exercise this choice without a second thought.

Ask Yourself This:

Was I the class clown in high school? Was I disruptive? What did I get out of playing this role? Did I feel good about myself? Did I believe that others liked me more? Did I feel accepted? Do I expect to have that same thing happen in college? Can I give up being the center of attention? Am I ready to act like an adult?

Think This:

I need to create a good reputation with my profs and peers in college. I had fun in high school, but it's time now to get serious and figure out how to be witty, engaging, or charismatic without being over-the-top.

Not That:
> I'm getting a lot of attention and this is going to keep me popular like I was in high school.

You will be popular, but this time, for all the wrong reasons. You won't see other students talking about your craziness, but they *will*, either to each other or to the prof. The press you get from what you're saying or doing won't be good.

Say This (to yourself)*:*
> I'm ready to give up the act and find my new self in college. People will like me for who I am. I can still be funny, but I don't have to be disruptive.

And Say This to Your Prof:
> ...if you've already displayed interesting behavior in class:

> I've done some distracting things in class and I apologize.

You don't need to add anything else. Your prof will understand what you're trying to say. If he has something else to add about your behavior, he'll do so. Listen and try not to get defensive. Reiterate that you will be a more focused, attentive student.

Not That:
> I've already acted kind of stupid, so I probably can't do anything to change anyone's opinion anyway.

Not true. Make tomorrow a new day. Go to class and act friendly without trying to disrupt the class. Be engaged. Use your wit to help the professor instead of challenging authority. Your peers and profs will appreciate the shift, even if they don't respond positively right away. They may want to see if this new you will stick before they reach out.

The End Note

The situation with Jake and Marshall didn't turn around the way I'd hoped and my class suffered. I had no other option but to talk to their soccer coach. I told him "I want to work this out myself. What can you tell me that might help?"

The coach assured me he'd have Jake and Marshall meet with me again, but that meeting never happened.

Before class the next day, Jake said, "You ratted us out!"

Crap. I thought the coach and I had an understanding.

"I didn't rat you out at all. Your coach does a monthly progress check (which was true), and I felt I had no choice but to ask his advice on what to do."

Jake spoke, but Marshall stood by, arms folded. "We've been told not to open our mouths again in your class."

Apparently, too many complaints were launched by other professors and even students. The previous week, Jake entered his psych class doing tumblesaults. Now their positions on the soccer team were at risk. So from that point forward, Jake and Marshall reluctantly participated when necessary, volunteered when they had to, and stared at the wall the rest of the time. Of course, their silence made teaching easier for me, but that particular class never reached any kind of relaxed climate.

My heart felt heavy over the situation. My goal was not to squelch the athletes' energy. Behind the fun and games were two excellent speakers—not a complete surprise due to their comfort with public displays. Had their behavior not spoken so loudly, they had a lot of value to add to our class.

Unfortunately, Jake and Marshall entered college, but hadn't mentally left high school. While they did pass my class, their grades were much lower than they could have achieved.

If you are some version of Jake or Marshall, face the reality about what being the class joker means for you in college: Students at this level don't tolerate immaturity among their peers. I've never had a disruptive student who wasn't criticized openly or privately by other students.

This is college.

The other people in your class left high school behind. Decide you're ready to find the grown-up version of yourself and follow them. I bet you'll find a whole new level of funny and your personality will shine!

Chapter 3

What Other Students Think and Feel

What You Might Say:

Everybody's confused about that writing assignment.

What Your Professor Thinks:

Telling me how other students feel doesn't help you.

The Real Story

Outspoken, outgoing Valeria came to see me during office hours. She entered my office in a huff and plopped down in the recliner next to my desk. (Full disclosure. The recliner isn't mine; it's my colleague's. He let me borrow it out of sympathy when I was pregnant a few years ago. It's a cushy recliner. Think light blue velvet like you'd see in your grandmother's house).

"I really don't get the requirements for this persuasive speech," Valeria said.

I wait for a second or two like an expectant puppy ... hoping she'll give me a little more information, but she doesn't. Finally, I asked, "Can you be more specific? What is it that's confusing you?"

"I don't get where we're supposed to refute opposition. I'm confused about the format." She paused for a minute. "And you know what? A bunch of other people are frustrated and confused, too. We needed more time to go over the structure of this speech in class."

I responded, "I appreciate you telling me about *your* confusion, Valeria, and I'm sorry you're frustrated. Let's break down the format so we can get you moving ahead on this speech and feeling good about it."

The Back Story

Students come to me with all sorts of personal issues: Megan had a death in the family. She now raises her young siblings and barely has time to do any school work, yet desperately wants to finish college. Hiro feels uncomfortable speaking out in the classroom because this is not typical in his Taiwanese culture. He'd rather e-mail me his thoughts privately. Alec just finished a tour of duty in Iraq and can't stop drinking.

While students often share their own problems openly, they rarely, if ever, talk about *another* student's personal lives. The same does NOT ring true when a student has a class-related problem. Then, the student suddenly becomes a spokesperson for every other person who shares the same complaint.

Of course, students don't tell me *who* is having the problem, so when I hear, "A bunch of other people don't understand this assignment either," I'm not exactly sure how many "a bunch" is. It could be two students, or fifteen, or maybe the whole class is confused. Maybe I've perplexed the entire college!

I certainly understand the spokesperson's need to sound like she's crowd-supported. After all, complaining to a prof feels scary, and even a little embarrassing when the student believes she *should* understand the information. Likewise, some students feel angry over an assignment or grade and want the professor to know that many other students share their opinion.

I absolutely want students to come to me for help. I'd much prefer students e-mail me or visit me every single day than silently suffer. Sure, I know students talk to each other and voice their frustrations about grades, work, and, yes, even about me. However, when a student is sitting in front of me, I can only help *that* student with his own problem. Think about it: Even if the student polled everyone in the class and every single one of their classmates agreed they didn't like something, I can't help everyone through one student. What's that spokes-student going to do? Return to the class with a megaphone and say, "I handled the problem. We're all good now!"

Let's say a bunch of Valeria's classmates don't understand the persuasive speech format. It's a tough project, so the fact that more than one student is struggling doesn't surprise me. However, if Valeria tells me that people are confused about the format, then that's too vague a statement for me. Some students might not understand opposition/refutation. Others might not know what to do with the visualization step. And a few may not know how to handle transitions. Everyone's "confusion over the format" may look very different. This is why I need to hear from individual students about their own points of frustration, confusion, or concern.

Another thought: If a flurry of students swarm into my office needing assistance, those masses will tell me I need to give more instructions for the assignment, or give more time for the assignment.

When I put the situation in this perspective, do you see why each individual voice can create a greater collective, positive change in the classroom?

Ask Yourself This:

Why am I telling my prof everyone else is confused? Do I feel embarrassed about the fact that I'm not getting it? Do I feel the prof won't take me seriously?

Have I previously told teachers about how others think and feel so I can have more basis for my own argument? Did saying this make any difference in getting help for myself?

Think This:

Hearing that my classmates are also confused makes me feel like I'm not totally clueless or going crazy. But even though we're all in the same boat, only the prof can get each of us unstuck and moving forward. Also, I can and should only vouch for myself. If my classmates are struggling, they should go to the prof and get individual help, too.

I know it's validating to know you aren't totally alone in your frustration. However, talking to your colleagues doesn't break you out of the confusion bubble. That's your prof's job.

Not That:

If I tell my prof everyone is confused, I won't look like the only one. The prof will think it's a big problem.

The moment a student tells me how everybody feels, he actually waters down his own need for help, and his peers miss an opportunity to use their own voice to get personalized assistance.

Say This:

Professor, I'm confused about our upcoming persuasive speech format.

Then be specific about what you're struggling with: "I'm having trouble figuring out if my thesis statement will work. I'm also not sure where the transitions go, and I don't know how to insert my opposition in the right place."

After you get the help you need, you can also say to your prof,

That makes far more sense to me now. Maybe you can share this with the whole class in case others are confused.

The prof will likely agree with you. Then, say to your colleagues, "If you're not sure about what's going on, go talk to the professor during office hours. I did and was able to get just what I needed to move ahead on this assignment."

Not That:

Everybody else isn't getting this either!

Or,

I know a bunch of other students also don't like the way this was explained.

The second you bring up how everyone else feels/thinks, you've just taken time—and credibility—away from getting help for yourself. This is one time when being self-centered and focusing on what *you* need is absolutely okay.

The End Note

In college, you don't need to represent the opinions of others. You only need to represent yourself. Your thoughts and concerns matter, regardless of whether anyone else shares them. There is power in numbers, but in this case, far more power in *individual* numbers. Explain your personal concerns and encourage your classmates to do the same.

Then, you can come together again to help each other.

Chapter 4

Distracting Classroom Behavior (Texting!)

What You May Think:

The professor is so busy talking, she isn't paying attention to me whispering, texting, or passing notes.

What Your Professor Thinks:

I can see everything that happens in my class, even when I'm knee-deep in a lecture. So can everyone else around you. You're either going to distract me ... or them.

The Real Story

Giancarlo and Niema engaged in what looked like an involved conversation during one of my evening classes. This wouldn't have bothered me, except I was trying to carry on a larger class discussion at the same time. Most profs view the buzz of side chatter like a fly that keeps darting around your head and you just can't swat it away.

I didn't call the duo out immediately (I'll explain how I typically handle these situations in a minute), but when my hints didn't stop their conversation, I sharply said, "Please stop!"

That worked.

We moved on to an activity and as I walked around the class, I noticed Niema had tears in her eyes. I asked if she was okay. She nodded. After class, she left quickly. I went up to Giancarlo and asked him what was going on.

He said, "She was embarrassed that we got called out." Giancarlo didn't apologize for the talking. It didn't sound like he apologized to Niema either.

I e-mailed Niema later and said, "It seems you were having an in-depth conversation, and it became very distracting. I didn't mean to upset you, but I didn't see that the talking was going to stop."

Niema e-mailed back and said, "I'm very sorry. Giancarlo kept talking to me."

Deferring the blame to the other person wasn't the best strategy to use, but I did appreciate Niema's apology. We could have avoided the entire thing if both students cut their conversation short and paid attention to what was going on in class!

Let me share another all-too familiar example: Texting in class.

Delia was a student who contributed to class discussion and seemed to have a good handle on our concepts and assignments. Grete sat next to Delia, but for whatever reason, the two barely spoke to each other.

One day we were discussing concepts from our listening chapter and I said, "When I was in college, I had a hard time staying focused. I *wanted* to listen to my professors, I knew I *needed* the information, I just couldn't force myself to pay attention."

Grete exclaimed, "And *some* people can't listen because they're texting." She looked right at Delia. She might have even pointed at her.

Yep. Delia was a total texter. I could see her hiding her phone under the desk, tapping away. She sat in front of the class, so her actions were unavoidable. Interestingly, Delia never checked out or seemed oblivious to what was going on. She asked thoughtful questions and initiated great responses to mine.

You can imagine Delia's mortification over being called out by Grete. "I don't think this is any of your business," she shot back.

Grete flared, "It is my business because it's disrespectful to the professor, and it's distracting to me."

Delia looked like she was about to cry. Not, "Boo hoo, I'm so embarrassed," but "Damn you, Lady, I'm so angry I can't think straight."

A few other students looked like they could cry, too. I think Grete made students feel guilty even if they never texted in class. The entire room grew uncomfortably quiet. Delia kept looking up and shaking her head, trying—not well—to conceal her emotions.

I told the women we should discuss the matter privately. I knew the class was looking to me to call Delia out, as well.

Did I know Delia texted during class? Of course. Anyone paying any shred of attention could see that. Because Delia's texting didn't take her away from our class, I didn't make a big deal out of it. Or, let's call it like it is: I didn't make any deal out of it.

Obviously, at least one other student thought Delia's texting was a *very* big deal.

The Back Story

Most class disruptions used to be generic: A little whispering here and there, note passing, side-talking, doodling, even doing other work instead of classwork. Several years ago, a student e-mailed me outing *himself*: "Ms. Bremen, I'm sorry I worked on my Political Science homework during your class the other day." I didn't see this student working on his Poly Sci homework, but I appreciated his honesty.

Now, technology has taken the generic classroom distractions to a whole new level: Texting, vibrating cell phones, iPhone games, Angry Birds ... the threats to student attentiveness are endless.

Professors aren't blind to students who behave in a distracting way or become distracted by something else, even when we seem completely absorbed in a lecture, a PowerPoint presentation, or a class discussion. Not only are we affected by distraction and disruption, but so are students. Maybe you've experienced this, yourself.

As a prof, how I wish I could un-see so much of what I do see. I *always* know when students are texting, passing notes, playing cell phone games, doing other work, sleeping in a corner, whispering, giggling, or eating (the eating, I actually don't mind—a little Frito's bag crinkle doesn't bother me, as long as someone isn't giving a speech).

Many educators are comfortable public speakers. We train ourselves to look at all parts of the room, make eye contact, and analyze our audience. For students, this means we have eyes all over, and we can see everything.

Even if I can't actually see students engaging in distracting behavior, I sense it. No, I don't have special powers (because that would just be freaky) but I can feel when the class's energy changes or when a section of the room becomes too quiet.

Think about it: When two students whisper or pass notes, those who sit around them will ultimately take notice and *their* attention is diverted. So, any prof tuned in to the mood of his class is going to notice.

You probably know from high school that professors differ in how they handle class disruptions. Some believe a disrupter *deserves* to be embarrassed and made an example of. Other professors take a quieter approach, standing close to the student to send a nonverbal message: *Stop what you're doing.*

Personally, I will not make eye contact with the disrupters—at least not at first. I say "Shhhh!" loudly in the air, hoping those who need the message will get it. If that doesn't work, I make direct eye contact and say something like, "Okay, shh, shh, shh... come back to me." If the problem continues, I zoom in on the offenders and say, "Please stop." Usually that works, but if it doesn't, then I talk to the students right after class or call a break in order to speak with them privately.

Similar to the situation with class jokers, dealing with disruptive, distracting students is exhausting and frustrating for a professor. We want to maintain a certain class rhythm. When I'm perpetually monitoring students' behavior, my concentration is thrown off. I imagine students who want to learn feel exactly the same way.

Finally, most profs work to create a friendly class environment. After turning into the distraction police, it's hard going right back to Ms. Flowers and Sunshine. My annoyance can infect the rest of the class time, which flat-out sucks. No other way to say it.

You can only *imagine* the class mood after the Grete-Delia situation. I admit I made a big error there. I should have dealt with Delia's texting earlier, but I didn't because, like I said, she was contributing in class. I didn't consider whether her texting bothered Grete or anyone else.

Based on this situation, I changed my texting policy in my syllabus. I added a new policy asking students to please refrain from texting in class, and if they need to text (or answer their phone), they must step out of class.

If you Google *texting in class*, you'll find many different perspectives on this subject. Some profs are much like me: If the texting isn't constant and doesn't seem disruptive to anyone, the prof overlooks it. Other profs give their students freedom to text during the entire class. These profs figure students will pay a natural heavy consequence for their choice to not pay attention. Other professors walk a hard line about texting in class and don't even want to see a phone out of a student's pocket, backpack, or purse.

You definitely need to find out where your prof stands on the texting issue before you pull out your phone. Better yet, if you're there to learn (you are, right?), then you probably know I'm going to say the texting can wait.

If you're expecting an important text or call, then set your phone to vibrate and put it in your pocket. If the message comes in, step out of class with as little noise as possible, and take care of business. Do not text under the desk (people can totally see you), and by all means, do *not* talk on your phone under the desk either (Yes, students do this, which looks as crazy as it sounds. Like the class isn't going to notice!).

Another thing you should know is that if you do step out of class, depending on your prof's attendance policy and the length of time you're gone, you may get dinged for not being present. So, again, take care of what you need to ... and then get back into class.

Ask Yourself This:

How often do I distract myself or others in classes by passing notes, doodling, doing unrelated class work, or whispering to others? Have I missed important information because of this? What causes me to do this? Am I bored, hungry, or confused?

With respect to texting: Why am I texting in class? Is this something I only do once in a while, or do I have a habit of texting all the time? Have I considered how texting affects others around me? Have I thought about what my professor thinks of me if I'm texting in class? If I'm honest with myself, could my texts wait until after class so I'm not distracted?

Think This:

This class is only 50 minutes (or an hour, or an hour and a half). I need to focus so I can get the most out of the time. I don't want to put myself behind because I couldn't pay attention. I know it's disrespectful to my classmates and to the prof if I do other things. Even if the class is boring, I'm going to focus and then reward myself later by doing something fun.

And back to texting:

Even if my professor doesn't have a policy on texting, I should keep my phone out of reach while I'm in class. If I hear a signal for a text, I'm going to be tempted to see what's going on. I'm only in this class for an hour and I can text later. If I'm in class longer than an hour, there will probably be a break and the texting can wait until then.

Not That:

If the prof made the class less boring, I'd be more likely to pay attention.

The prof won't notice what I do and other students won't care.

It's my class time. I'm paying for it, and I'll spend it however I want to.

You can take certain steps to deal with a boring class (See Chapter 33), instead of distracting yourself. Just as students are often bothered by the disruption of class jokers, you'd be surprised how many of your fellow students are frustrated by whispering, texting, and other disturbances. That irritation is warranted! You're paying for this education (or someone is paying for it). Don't you want to get your money's worth? Even if you don't, you're part of a community. Your peers may not agree that you can spend the class time however *you* want if it distracts *them* from learning.

Or,

I'll just text quickly and tell the person I'm in class.

One follow up question could throw you into a conversation. Don't risk it unless you're 100 percent sure you won't get sucked in. The ramifications aren't worth it.

Say This:

If your prof has called you out or commented privately about your distracting behavior, go up to her after the class and say,

I'm very sorry about my behavior today. I didn't mean to be disruptive or disrespectful and I won't let it happen again.

And don't. If another student is trying to distract you...

Then say (or write),

Hey, I'll be glad to chat after class. Looks like the prof is watching us.

You can also say,

I'm waiting to see if the prof is going to give us more information about the upcoming test (assignment, whatever). I don't know about you, but I need it.

Then turn your full attention to the prof. Or, if you have an emergency and need to watch for a text or call, say (to your professor),

> My mom needs me to pick my brother up from school if her car isn't ready. She said she'd text me by 11 o'clock. I told her I would be in class at that time, but I'll watch to see what's happening. If I have to step out of class for a minute, I wanted you to know why.

Otherwise, if your professor calls you out for texting, stop doing it immediately and put your phone away. Then, after class, talk to your prof privately and say,

> I'm sorry for texting in class. I didn't mean to be disrespectful. I made a mistake and I won't let happen again.

(You can say the same thing to a fellow student who found your texting distracting.)

Not That:
> I wasn't doing anything wrong,

Or,
> Joe was texting me.

If your prof has to tell you to be quiet or stop whatever you're doing, either openly or in private, then defensiveness is a bad idea. He already feels disrespected by your actions. Don't make things worse. Be humble and apologetic.

The End Note

Are you wondering what happened with Grete and Delia?

I apologized to Grete for not handling the situation sooner and for being oblivious to the fact that the texting bothered her. I did say it might have been better had she come to me or spoken to Delia privately, and that I was concerned about their ability to be civil to each other in class. Grete promised she would attempt to smooth the situation over, but stood by her opinion that Delia was inconsiderate.

I also spoke to Delia: "I really appreciate how much you contribute in class, and I know you're up to speed on what we're working on. That's why I haven't made an issue of your texting. I made a mistake, though, because I didn't consider how it might affect others."

Delia became defensive. "Grete had no right to say anything, especially in front of the whole class! I'm not doing anything to her!"

"I agree we should have discussed it between us if there was a problem. I'm sorry it came out that way, and I want the two of you to be able to function in class together. In the meantime, I do need to ask you to stop texting in class. If you have something you need to take care of, step out of the classroom for a moment."

Delia wasn't thrilled with the discussion, but she agreed.

Grete ended up having a medical situation and didn't finish the class. Delia completed the class and did well. I don't believe the two students ever patched things up, which is unfortunate.

Ironically, in an entirely different class, my student, Misty, came to me and said, "Ellen, I don't mean to complain, but I notice a lot of texting going on while people are giving speeches. It's distracting and I wonder if you can make an announcement for people to put their phones away on speech nights."

I hadn't seen any texting while I was teaching, and while students are giving speeches, my attention is focused on the speaker, writing notes on my evaluation form, and glancing around the class every so often to make sure no one is sleeping or talking. Students absolutely do see things I don't, and I was glad Misty came to me, rather than having an outburst.

Both of these situations were huge learning moments for me: I realized I need to be more aware of texting in my classroom and its effect on students. I'm sure I'm not alone in that. Your prof may be dealing with the issue, too, and trying to figure out what to do, short of making everyone leave their cell phones in a basket at the door (Could you imagine them all going off at once? Holy ringtone, Batman!).

So, on behalf of all students, I ask you to help a professor out. Think about your texting behavior in class (and any other distracting behavior you might exhibit) and try to avoid it. The problem is definitely becoming worse as texting eclipses other forms of communication. If your texter gets annoyed because you didn't respond, blame it on your prof not letting you text in class.

We can take it.

Remember: You're in college to attend classes, learn from your profs and your colleagues, and build relationships with others. Distracting yourself takes you from the experience and, practically speaking, you will probably miss important class information.

I get that sometimes you *want* to be taken away because you're bored. We've all been there and we all go through it. There will be times in your professional life when you have to sit through long, boring meetings. As a student or an employee, getting caught doing other things makes you appear disinterested and creates a negative impression.

Work with self-discipline now to train yourself for later. Class is a finite period of time. Make a deal with yourself to pay attention and be engaged with your professor and with others—or engaged in the never-ending lecture. You can reward yourself later with a movie, a magazine, a candy bar, whatever ... because you stayed focused.

Chapter 5

Comparing Grades With Others

What You Might Say:

Joe got a 92 and I only got an 88, but we have the same check marks on our score sheet.

What Your Professor Thinks:

Asking why you didn't get what Joe got is the fast track to misery for both of us.

The Real Story

Polina came to see me during office hours with a graded assignment in hand.

"I don't understand it," she said. "Why did I get an 88 and someone else got a 92? The other person has fewer comments than I do."

"I can't discuss anyone else's grade with you," I replied. "But I'd be glad to take a closer look at your grade and see what put you into the B range."

Another student, Clint, caught me after class a few days later. "I'm pretty okay with the grade I got," he said, "but I heard a bunch of speeches I thought were a lot worse than mine."

"Are you saying that because you want to discuss the grade you received?" I asked.

"No. I know why I got what I did."

"Are you sure?" I pressed. "I'm definitely glad to go over it with you."

Clint still refused. He received a high C due to strong delivery of his speech, but his content needed considerable work. That particular class received more C's on speeches than usual, so I never fully identified what grade Clint was comparing his own to.

The Back Story

When I was a student, I compared, too. How can you resist? You get that grade back from your prof and the temptation is thick like marshmallow crème. You're dying to know: Did your classmates do better than you? Did the person who wrote that paper at the last minute get the grade you think he deserved? (You hope so!). Did the person who bombed their assignment do worse then you? (Again, you hope so!).

Rob Walsh, one of my favorite communication colleagues (and one my favorite people, just in general), has a saying about "What'd you get?" on his syllabus, and I adopted it for my own:

Comparison is the fast track to misery.

Did comparing make me miserable when I was a student? Yes! Especially when I didn't get the grade I thought I deserved, and someone else did.

Does comparing make me miserable as a prof? Hell, yes! I'm in a field that seems to breed vague grading. If I taught math, the answers would be much more exact (but I wouldn't know them anyway because math isn't my strong subject).

To ease some of the subjectivity in my grading, I use rubrics to make the process as transparent as possible. These rubrics are always available to students before assignments. I want everyone to know what to expect. Likewise, you should know what's expected from your work so you can figure out which grade you'd like to achieve.

Let's say you get a grade that isn't what you anticipated. You discover someone else did better than you, but they have fewer comments. Or, their rubric/checklist/score sheet seems to contain more comments, but their grade is still higher. I'll give an example of how this can happen: In my class, a student can earn a C on a speech for a variety of reasons:

- Decent delivery, but leaving out two of three required sources
- Reading 70 percent of the speech, but the content is mostly solid
- Going short on time (more than a minute), leaving out one source, decent delivery
- Going long on time, tedious delivery (reading, lots of stalls), decent content

The breakdown for my informative speech is 70 points for content and 30 points for delivery. If a student reads her entire speech, she can fail the delivery portion of the grade. My syllabus even states that this is a Communication Studies department policy.

So with the 70/30 breakdown of points, if delivery or content is suffering, two students could earn a C for different reasons. Now let's say one went over her speaking time, which knocks off 5 more points. Both scores change again for entirely different reasons.

Students can only fully understand why they receive a certain grade if I offer specific comments. Circling numbers on a rubric/checklist/score sheet can't give the whole story. When a student comes to me all pissed over their low grade versus someone else's higher grade, I always refer the student back to my comments. I reiterate why his grade was lower and what led to that determination.

I tell the student his grade is never, ever based on the best work in the class. It would be highly unfair to grade students against each other's work, rather than...

a) their own individual mastery (or lack thereof) of the assignment's requirements; and,

b) their individual improvement on that assignment, if relevant.

No matter how many times I tell students this, they still compare their work with others in class, then judge themselves. You have nothing positive to gain from comparing, unless you genuinely feel good knowing you did better than others. But if you don't get that answer, what then? You'll probably feel a lot worse.

What should you do? Get the facts. If your classroom work doesn't have fixed answers (like research papers, projects, etc.), it's critical to find out how you'll be graded. Always ask for anything you can get that describes how the prof grades, such as a checklist, rubric, score sheet, or examples of other students' work. You need this *before* your work is turned in. Once you follow these guidelines and read the feedback from your prof, hopefully the reason for your grade will become clear.

If you're unclear about your grade, *the only person who can answer your questions is the person who graded you.* Your classmates can commiserate with you, make you feel better, or make you feel worse (particularly if their grades were higher), but they can't give you concrete reasons why your grade is what it is.

Silently seething is no better. If you're angry or frustrated with your professor, you'll have a hard time paying attention, you'll dread going to class, and your work may suffer. You're paying for this education. Feeling frustrated for an extended period of time isn't what you're paying for. Your professor is your partner in education, not your adversary, though at times you may feel that way.

Ask Yourself This:

What do I hope to learn when I ask others about their grades? Am I trying to make myself feel better? How will I handle it if I feel worse? What have I felt in the past when I compared my grades with others in my class? Did knowing make me feel better? Did I take action based on what I learned? Did the action help me?

Think This:

My grade is the only one that matters. If I'm not happy with my grade, finding out others' grades isn't going to change my frustration. I can take control of this situation, go to the prof, and discuss what's bothering me about this grade. If I do choose to ask others about their grades, or if they happen to tell me, I can't let this information impact my own possibilities for success.

Not That:

The prof likes Monica better than me, which is why she got a better grade.

Believe it or not, profs do not grade on personality.

I'm not as smart as Reynaldo and that's why I didn't do as well.

The fact that someone else received a better grade does *not* reflect how intelligent you are. An undesirable grade is a reflection of work based on a series of set requirements—not your abilities as a person.

Say This:

Before the assignment, if these items are not available to you, say,

Do you have any rubrics, samples, checklists, examples, or further explanations of how you'll be grading our work?

You may also say,

Will you review work in advance? How early do you need to receive my draft?

You might say,
> I'd like more specific feedback on what lowered my score for this assignment.

If you absolutely cannot resist the urge to admit you saw someone else's grades, then you can say, "I know it isn't a good idea to compare my grade with others, but I happen to know Selwyn got a 92. I thought I did at least as well as he did on this assignment. Can you explain why my grade was lower?"

Disclaimer! In the spirit of confidentiality, the prof can only discuss *your* grade with you. She can't talk about anyone else's score or the quality of their work, so if you bring it up, you won't be able to get the answers you want about the other student's grade.

Not That:
> I don't understand why three other people got a higher grade than I did. What did they do that I didn't?

Remember, lead with your concerns about *your* grade. Being confrontational and asking about someone else's grade sends the message you believe the professor is unfair. You want to maintain a positive relationship, and even if you're upset over your grade, you want to handle it in a professional way.

End Note

Even as I suggest you shouldn't wonder about other people's grades, I know it's human nature to do so. Even if you don't ask about others' grades, you may find out anyway if someone tells you. Regardless, remember my dear friend Rob's phrase: Comparison *is* the fast track to misery.

Don't make yourself miserable. Focus on *your* grades and your grades alone.

If someone tries to bring you into his grade world, encourage him to do the same thing you'll be doing from now on: Make an appointment with the prof and get the full story.

Chapter 6

"Getting" Grades and Working "Hard" for Your Grades

What You Might Say:

I got a D? Why'd you *give* me that grade?

Or,

I worked *so* hard on that paper! I should have an A!

What Your Professor Thinks:

You weren't given a grade. You earned it. Your hard work doesn't guarantee you any grade.

The Real Story

Leslie's work fell short of requirements time and time again.

She turned in her assignments for early review, but didn't follow my recommendations for full improvement. For example, when I told Leslie her persuasive speech topic was too informative, she became defensive and said on a discussion board to her peers, "I've never gotten anything helpful from the prof, not even that I have a good topic." When I told Leslie she didn't have enough sources for her speech, she added them, but ended up taking huge chunks of information from her citations, rather than paraphrasing the content and incorporating it with *her* ideas. This could be seen as a form of plagiarism. With her work perpetually missing the mark in terms of sources, content, and overall accuracy, Leslie received a final grade of a C-, which I actually considered a win for her.

Leslie didn't see it that way. She became angry and said, "I don't deserve for you to *give* me a C! I worked *hard* in this class!"

Let's talk about another student, Samad. Samad's work was always on-point, and if not, he made quick and accurate changes. Samad scored highly on his outlines and other written work. His speeches were mostly well-delivered, except for going over time twice (which only reduced his grade by 5 points each time, a standard in many speech classes). Samad received an A. After the class was over, he e-mailed me and said, "I enjoyed your class and I want to thank you for giving me an A."

Ready for one last example? Let's talk about Tierra, who showed up at my office door while I was finalizing grades. I noticed a ScanTron in her hand as I let her in.

"I got a terrible grade on my final!" Tierra exclaimed. "My grade dropped to a C because of it. I was doing pretty well in this class. I had a B and then I took this final and now I'm going to get a C in the class."

She stopped for a moment, then continued. "You know, I worked very hard in this class. I studied and studied for the final. I finished all of my quizzes. I read the book. I don't know what happened."

"I'm not sure either," I replied. "Why don't we look at your grades one-by-one and see if we can figure it out."

As it turned out, Tierra's grade was the result of many small, missed points here and there. The low final exam grade, while only worth 35 percent, was just enough to slip her down to a C. She didn't have enough A's to average out the lower C grades.

The Back Story

Each of these situations is based on the idea that grades are a random event: that grades are given away, or hard work somehow guarantees them, rather than the fact that grades are tied to...

a) the quality of a student's work,

b) course requirements, or

c) other concrete events.

I seriously wonder if students think I calculate grades by throwing darts, plucking grades out of a hat, or playing Pin the Tail on the GPA.

Let's go back to Leslie and Samad: In neither of these cases did I *give* students their grades; these students *earned* their grades. And, sure,

Leslie worked hard. So did Samad and Tierra, for that matter. But hard work doesn't instantly create a grade.

Let's examine that "hard work equals a high grade" idea for a moment, in a slightly different direction: I've struggled with weight all my life. My mother has almost always been very obese, as were each of her parents. I was on the same path until 1998, when I lost 90 pounds over a period of four years. Except for my pregnancies, the fight continues to this day.

If you've ever tried to lose weight, you know you can bust your ass exercising, eat the right things, then step on the scale and not lose a pound (or worse, gain a pound). Or, you can exercise, eat terribly and not lose a thing, but *believe* you're working hard at dieting. Weight loss is the perfect example of hard work never guaranteeing an outcome.

Like a physician who has no idea what you're *really* putting in your mouth or if you're hitting your target heart rate during exercise, your prof can't see into your house with a telescope to log all your study hours. So, how can your prof possibly reward you for effort?

Also, let's say you *did* work extremely hard. You memorized your textbook and could practically write a new one. Sometimes strange things happen in the transition from learning to doing. I know there were times when I felt ready for a test, a speech, even a half-marathon. Then, the big day came and I bit it—and not in a good way. Yes, I worked hard, but when the moment of truth arrived, my hard work didn't pay off. I'd have to try again.

Finally, hard work has different meanings, doesn't it? Some students believe 30 minutes of studying is medal-worthy. Others believe studying every waking hour isn't enough.

I realize students feel embarrassed when they do poorly. So, they defend themselves by puffing up and saying how much effort they expended. But, sadly, because *effort* is based on individual opinions, professors can't pay too much attention to your proclamations about it.

Now let's get to the inside scoop on grading. As you can imagine, it's a crazy-complex part of a prof's job. I'm sure many of my colleagues agree it's one of the most stressful parts of our job. Even with the most specific feedback and glaring evidence, students experience every emotion from slightly perturbed to on-the-ceiling outrage when they disagree with a grade.

Unfortunately, too few students take responsibility for grades they *earn*. Instead, students blame the prof for what they believe was given *to* them. These irate students share their fury with anyone who'll listen. What many students rarely do is look inward and ask: "What could *I* have done differently to earn a better grade?"

As I said, grading is a complex process. A great deal of thought and background work occurs in order for you to get your grades. I'll explain:

Look at any course syllabus and you'll probably find a section called Course Objectives or Outcomes. For a professor, objectives are an academic way of saying "Here's what I want my students to know or be able to do at the end of this course." Sometimes, your prof writes the objectives; sometimes a department or college writes the objectives. Regardless, objectives are the starting point for your prof to identify what he/she should teach you during the term and what you'll be tested on.

Assignments and tests enter the picture because your professors need to measure how well you know, or can perform, what you've learned. These tools let you show what you know, and your professor uses points or a letter grade to tell you where you excel and where your performance needs more work.

How do these assignments and tests happen? Many profs create them on their own, with much thought and research in the process. We look at other professors' exams and assignments. We review curriculum from textbooks and instructor's manuals. We ask colleagues from all over the country what they're having students do. We gain new ideas from conferences and the organizations we belong to. Some profs keep the same assignments and exams for years; other profs change them every term. Some departments even analyze tests (down to the question) and assignments regularly, calculating student scores and reflecting on ways the instruction could improve. So, as you can see, your profs are not just giving you work to do. Mental Olympics go into choosing your classwork.

Now let's look at grades from your point of view: The syllabus probably lists assignments and exams you'll have to complete. Ultimately, you make the decision about how much or how little effort you'll put into this work. If you choose to do your 10-page research paper 48-hours before it's due and you end up with a D because you only wrote eight pages and didn't have the correct sources, then you chose to *earn* that grade. Your professor didn't randomly *give* it. Instead, your professor considered the criteria for the actual assignment and then reviewed your paper based on how well you met the requirements.

Let's say you worked your butt off on the paper, met all the requirements, and received an A. You worked to earn *that* grade. I won't deny many students work hard and then receive lower grades than they expected. If that happens to you, I can guarantee your prof didn't pull this grade out of the air. Your professor is obligated to tell you why you earned the grade.

You know what? You also have a right to know how you'll be graded before your grade ever happens. How? You can ask for rubrics, samples of student work, checklists, scoring sheets, or other data. Your syllabus might have information, too, such as "If you want an A in this class, you will do the following..."

I'm going to tell you how to ask for these documents so you have the best chance to earn the grade you want. You may run into a professor who doesn't have any rubrics or samples to give you. This person may be new to the classroom and frankly doesn't know what he's looking for. If that's the case, I'll show you other ways to get the information you need, but you have to ask *early*—preferably at least two weeks before the assignment is due—never two days.

Ask Yourself This:

Why am I telling my prof how hard I worked on my test/studied for my assignment? Do I think my prof will raise my grade? Will she give me a chance to redo an assignment? Do I think just because I worked hard, I should automatically receive a high grade, even if I didn't fully meet the requirements of the assignment or the test?

When I receive a grade I'm not happy about, do I tend to blame others? Have I ever set a grade goal and found out what was required to reach that goal before the work was due?

Think This:

I can ask questions, get help, and find out specifics about what's expected of me. If I don't do well, I need to look at what I could have done better and ask for clarification. Maybe I didn't have a handle on the material like I thought I did. Maybe I should have submitted my work for early review. Maybe I didn't ask enough questions.

I'm supposed to work hard in college. Often, putting in a lot of quality study hours will result in the reward of high grades. But, sometimes I will work hard and still not earn the grades I hope for or expect. If I keep working hard, I will succeed, more often than not.

Not That:

The professor just gives whatever grades she feels like giving. It doesn't matter what I do or how hard I work. She's going to do what she wants.

He's giving me this grade because he doesn't like me.

My professor owes me because I put in a lot of time on this assignment. I should get an A for my effort.

A professor can't possibly grade you on "working your butt off" (What grade would that be—Worked Butt Off = WBO? Your profs have to grade you on tangible results: the requirements of an assignment and how well you mastered those requirements.)

Say This:

Well before the assignment is due:

I'd like to know how this assignment is graded. Do you have examples of what it takes to get an A, or a B, etc.? Do you have any rubrics, samples of student work, checklists, score sheets, or other documents that might help me?

If the professor says,

No, I'm sorry. I don't have anything available.

You can say,

Can you tell me what you'll be looking for? I'll write it down.

(You could even offer to type this list for the rest of the class—your prof may appreciate that).

If the professor still doesn't give clear guidance about what's expected...

You can say,

Are there other professors in the department who do a similar assignment? Would they have any student examples that could help?

(Remember, your professor may be new). If you don't feel comfortable making this request...

You can say,

> I'd like to do my work early and then have you look at it to make sure I'm on the right track. Can you give me some feedback? What's the last day you'll be willing to review?"

Once you get your work back, if you're concerned about your grade, say,

> I'm surprised and concerned about the grade I received. I was expecting it to be higher and believe I followed the requirements. Can you explain what needed to be done differently?

(Note: You only have the right to do this if you asked for information ahead of time and/or a review. If you did sub-par work to begin with, you don't have a leg to stand on.) If the professor is unclear about why you received the grade, check your syllabus to see if you have a similar assignment coming up.

Say,

> I see we have a similar assignment coming up and I'd like to do better next time. When should I have you review this work to make sure I'm on the right track?

Not That:

> You didn't tell us what was required and that's why I didn't do well!
> Why did you give me a C on this assignment?
> I worked so hard. Can't you give me some credit for that?

Blaming your prof won't get you anywhere, and your prof didn't give you anything. He cannot give you credit for trying, even if he's really, really impressed by your description of your effort.

The End Note

Get used to the idea that you'll need to show proof of your abilities. During the rest of your life, you won't be able to say, "I worked hard" and get credit for it.

You'll have to put real effort behind those words. Think about it: At your job, the only time you'll be able to get by on verbal examples of how hard you work is during your initial interview. After that point, you'll have to show your boss exactly what you can do. And you won't get a promotion or raise because you say, "But I worked really hard!"

Career rewards come from a proven track record—the deliverables that back up your solid work ethic. You know, your hard work!

So start doing it ... there's no need to talk about it.

You *do* have control over the grades you earn, even though sometimes you may feel like a victim of those grades.

Keep in mind that grading is as serious to your professors as it is to you. We do not use dartboards, Monopoly, or even GPA Uno.

Now if someone comes out with a version of Angry Birds where you can fling... Just kidding!

Chapter 7

A Zero Grade

What You Might Say:

I couldn't do that assignment. I'll just take the zero.

What Your Professor Thinks:

Any points are better than zero points.

The Real Story

My students had a 100-point journal assignment due, and Margot, Shalonda, Michael, and Lane did not submit it.

Margot contacted me and said she was confused about what to do and didn't ask for help early enough. Shalonda sent an e-mail saying her mother, who had been away from the family, had returned and was camping out in her living room. In light of this, she couldn't get the journal done. Michael had two employees at his job he needed to cover for and couldn't finish either. Lane had a chemistry exam that needed more of his time. He completed about 50 percent of the journal, but figured it wasn't worth turning in half.

Each of these students received a zero for the journal assignment. And for a 100-point assignment, a zero has the potential to reduce the overall course grade by a full letter.

Now, of course, not all zero grades come from work that is knowingly not submitted. Some zero grades come from assignments students *think* they've submitted, but were not actually received. That's right. In this day of papers and exams submitted electronically, technology can fail, and it often does! I've had many students shocked by a low final course grade, and when we analyze the individual points we realize an assignment was never graded because I didn't get it.

The Back Story

Let's start by talking about the students who knew that they didn't submit their work. Margot could get help, turn in her journal, and receive points for it. The sad truth is, far too many students *prefer to take a zero rather than ask for that help.* Helping is what your professors are there for, so giving *yourself* a zero grade rather than getting assistance—and points for your work—doesn't make much sense, does it?

Shalonda will likely turn in her journal late and receive a penalty. Her writing is strong, so the penalty could potentially be subtracted from an already high grade. The high grade, brought down by a late penalty, is far better than a zero.

Michael may or may not turn in his journal, so he could end up with that zero.

Lane could have submitted the completed section of the journal, received as many points as possible there, and then submitted the remaining 50 percent with a late penalty. He could have ended up with a possible B or a C.

Think about this: A missed assignment that earns zero points puts pressure on the remaining assignments. You'll need to earn high points in order to "average up" the zero scores—depending on what you're trying to earn in the class, of course.

I realize some profs have a policy allowing late submissions, with penalties. Others say, "No late work under any circumstances." Check your syllabus to find out which side of the policy your prof is on. If you can turn in work after the deadline and avoid the zero, then by all means talk to your prof, get the work done, and receive any points that are still possible. Even if your prof has a "no late work under any circumstances" policy, you can still ask and see if there's a chance to earn, well ... anything. There may not be, but you might be surprised.

Also keep in mind that if you've only completed part of an assignment by the due date, you might still receive some credit for it. *Turn it in.* If you didn't finish because you were confused, the prof needs to see what you've done in order to help you. If you didn't finish because of poor time management (just keeping things real here), then grab points for what you *did* accomplish. Do anything to avoid that zero.

Let's see how the calculations break down between the two students:

Lane		Shalonda	
Assignment 1	40/50	Assignment 1	50/50
Assignment 2	40/50	Assignment 2	40/50
Assignment 3	37/50	Assignment 3	45/50
Exam 1	80/100	Exam 1	90/100
Assignment 4	0/50 (not submitted)	Assignment 4	30/50 (late penalty)
Assignment 5	42/50	Assignment 5	50/50
Exam 2	79/100	Exam 2	85/100
TOTAL	318/450=71%	TOTAL	390/450=87%
With partial credit	348/450 = 77%	With the zero	360/450 = 80%

Those extra points make a difference, don't they?

Now let's talk about the other part of this scenario: You did the work and turned it in, but your professor never received it. You have a zero and didn't even know. The problem here is that too few students monitor their grades throughout a term. I'm shocked by how many students are blindsided by their grades at the end because they didn't keep tabs on them during the semester.

The solution is simple: Whenever you turn in an assignment, make sure it was received—especially if you submit electronically. If you have access to your grades in a course management system, *check them all the time* (how about right now? I'll wait...). Make sure you have credit for every single thing you've turned in and be sure the points are accurate.

Professors make mistakes.

I have transposed numbers.

I've missed inputting a grade, and then handed the student back his work.

I have put in the wrong grade.

This happens rarely, but it does happen, and that's why it's critical for you to always stay on top of your grades. If you come to the end of a term and find you have a zero that shouldn't be there because you did submit the assignment, then immediately get that assignment into your prof's hands. You can't waste any time because the prof may wonder if you just now completed it. Of course, this means you have to save and back up your work, always. And save the emails you send.

Ask Yourself This:

Why did I receive a zero grade? Did I not do the work because I was confused? Did I not manage my time to get it done? Was something missed that I did turn in? Do I have a history of receiving zero grades? How have those zeroes impacted my grades overall? How do I feel when I receive a zero on an assignment? Am I willing to ask for help or turn in late work to avoid zeroes? What has held me back from asking for help in the past?

Think This:

This isn't time for excuses or begging. I need to look at the late policy in the syllabus and see what points I can salvage. Even 20 points out of the 100 points is 20 points to add to the final grade.

And,

I'm going to stay on top of my grades, check them often, and make sure I don't have any zeroes I don't know about. I don't want to be surprised at the end of the term with a grade that's been brought down by a zero.

Not That:

The zero won't matter. I can bring up my grade in other assignments.

How do you know? What if it doesn't happen? You risk your final grade by putting pressure on all those other assignments. Get *something* for the work you've done—even if it's only a few points.

Or,

The prof has all my work and I'm sure she's giving me credit.

The prof may *not* have all your work and you may not have credit for what you've done. You want the credit, right? Of course, you do!

Say This:

After you review the syllabus and look at exactly how many points you can still receive by turning in the assignment late, contact your professor and say,

I'm sorry. My assignment is going to be submitted late. I reviewed the syllabus and see that since I'm going to be one week late, I'm eligible to only receive partial credit, which would be 50 out of 100 points. Can you please confirm if this is correct? I won't let this happen again.

You should also ask,
> Is the 50 points an automatic grade, or will I earn less than 50 points if there are issues with my work?

What you want to know, essentially, is if the 100 points you could have earned for the assignment on time is now reduced to a 50-point starting place. Professors handle this situation differently. Some will give you the partial credit since it's already technically a failing grade (but don't let that stop you. It's the points added to your final total that matter). Others will actually grade the work and apply your points from the new starting place, whether it's 50 points, 75 points, or whatever.

If there is no late policy, you want to ask,
> Can I receive any points at all for turning this work in?

If the answer is "Yes," graciously say,
> Thank you. When should I have this work in to you?

And make *sure* you don't miss that deadline. If you do, take the zero and move on without complaining.

When you submit late work, say,
> I turned in my assignment by the late deadline and want to make sure you received it.

(This can be via e-mail or in person).

You might also ask,
> I'd like to make sure my grades are correct and I don't have any zeroes I'm aware of. May I make an appointment with you to compare my records to yours?

If you didn't check your grades early enough and suddenly find you have a low overall grade, ask,
> My grade is lower than expected and I'm wondering if one of my assignments isn't in the gradebook. Can you check on this for me?

If your prof finds you do have a zero because she didn't receive your work, then say,
> I turned in that assignment and have a copy of it I can submit it to you immediately. I hope you'll still accept it and grade it. I apologize for not checking on this sooner. I'll be sure to check my grades far earlier.

If you have a record, such as an email or the course management system that shows you did submit the assignment, definitely provide this proof. But it may not be needed.

Not That:
Why is my grade so low?

First, ask yourself if you missed turning in an assignment. If so, you have a zero and that's the reason for the low grade. If you submitted everything, then something might have been missed, so ask about that specifically, rather than a blanket "What's wrong with my grade?"

The End Note
I hope, hope, hope you'll ask for help, rather than taking a zero on an assignment.

I hope, hope, hope you'll submit work that's even partially done, rather than no submission at all. Let the numbers speak for themselves. Any additional points can only help your grade.

No points can only hurt your grade.

The only right thing to do is—help your grade. Get *something* in the prof's hands (preferably, a well-done assignment).

Chapter 8

Getting the Grade You Need

What You Might Say:

But I really needed a 3.5 in this class so it will transfer to my program! (stated on week 10)

What Your Professor Thinks:

Ask what you can do to get the grade you need during week one, not week 14 when we can't do much about it.

The Real Story

I teach my Intro to Communication class on Wednesday nights. This is a long class, about three and a half hours, so I typically give the students a break mid-way.

On the first night, after going over the syllabus, we did a crazy activity that involves making a shape out of a pipe cleaner and interviewing another classmate. (In case you were wondering, yes, students typically think I'm on crack by this point. But the activity actually has deeper theoretical meaning about public speaking fears).

On the break, two students, Dimitry and Ana, approached me. Ana spoke first, "Um, when you were going over the syllabus, you said if we need a certain grade, we should tell you early. I need a 4.0."

Dimitry chimed in, "Me, too! What do we need to do?"

"Awesome! I'm glad to know your grade goals early!" I exclaimed. "Here's the plan."

For my class, I told Dimitry and Ana to focus on written work over the speeches because we can review those early, passing them back and forth via e-mail. Speeches are more of a done-deal and the written work is worth more points.

Dimitry and Ana seemed comfortable with my advice and said they'd take it. I could only hope they would follow through.

Now, let's hit fast-forward to the end of that same quarter, same class, two different students: Dane, whose final grade was a D, and Sarah, who earned a B.

Dane e-mailed and said, "So, is this the final grade? Is there anything I can do? I needed to do better than this."

Dane missed several small assignments, and those points added up. He didn't do well on his speech outlines, even though the speeches, when delivered, were slightly above average (but speeches and outlines are two separate grades). He never made arrangements with me for missed assignments or to figure out how to improve.

My response? "We needed to have this conversation at least eight weeks ago. We could have kept tabs on your grades throughout the course."

Sarah came to see me in my office. "You don't understand!" she cried. "I'm trying to get into pre-Pharmacy. I needed at least a 3.5 so this class will transfer."

Sarah's work was more solid than Dane's. She had great content but read much of her speech, rather than using conversational delivery. In other words, she was just shy of A-level work.

I repeated what I said to Dane: "Sarah, I really wish I'd known about your goals far earlier in the term. This was a conversation we needed to have on *the first day*, especially if there are high stakes, such as getting into another program."

Then Sarah blew me away. "I'll do anything," she said, sounding frantic. "I'll mow your lawn. I'll babysit your kids."

Ugh. Bribery. That was actually a new one after 13 years. (But it is hard to find a good babysitter these days ... kidding!)

Now I had to get firm. Bribery has no place in communication between a student and a professor. "Sarah, I realize you're feeling desperate right now," I said. "But what you're proposing is unethical, unprofessional, and not something a professor would or should ever accept. If we continue this dialogue, I'm going to have to bring my division chair in."

Wide-eyed and red-faced, Sarah shook her head and said, "No, no. I'm very sorry. I was just upset."

The Back Story

I felt for Sarah. When you don't plan, then feel blindsided by the result, you feel desperate to change the outcome. What's unfortunate is that every student who's shocked by a grade could have turned the situation around just by initiating a grade goal discussion *early*.

The message here is a no-brainer: Figure out the grade you want or need in the class and take responsibility for that grade during *the first day or first week of the term*. Do *not* wait until mid-term or later to ask what you need to do for the grade you want. Here's what will inevitably happen if you do:

Scenario 1: It isn't quite mid-term. You've received a few graded assignments from your prof. You aren't doing as well as you'd hoped, and you wonder how many points were possible for those assignments so you know where you stand. You panic, suddenly realizing you only have three more assignments, your mid-term, and a final examination left. An awful lot of pressure is riding on that work if you want to get a decent grade.

Scenario 2: You take the mid-term and your grade is horrible. You've gotten good grades (low A's, high B's) until that point, but a bad headache kept you from doing your best on the exam. It is worth twice the points of those smaller assignments. Now you're fearful about what will happen if you don't do well on the final and the remaining assignments.

Scenario 3: You reach the end of the term and finally pay attention to your overall grade picture. You add up your points, look at the points possible, and realize your goal grade of A, B, C or even a passing D, will not happen.

In all three of these situations, students may mildly sweat or completely freak. Then, the lost "I needed this grade" chat between student and professor that *should* have happened weeks before is suddenly an absolute emergency. Students' mental sirens blare; they hunt down the prof for an appointment or send a frantic e-mail either asking what they can still do to salvage a grade or, even worse, will angrily say, "You don't understand! I *needed* an A in this class!" The underlying message is that the professor should be reactive. It's up to *us* to try and clean up the grade mess the student caused by not starting this conversation earlier. As a professor, I hate being reactive. I am *so* much better at being proactive.

Before I tell you what to say, I'll offer what I hope will be a comforting thought: Your goal doesn't have to be a 4.0 in order to have this conversation with your prof. Profs know that students' grade ambitions vary. Some students seek the highest grades to attain and maintain scholarships. Other students are happy to pass with a midline grade, say a C or C minus. We don't pass judgment on your goals because they are totally personal to you and your own experience. The point is, whatever you're after, go for it. Don't wait until the grade happens to you. Don't think you're doing A or B work only to find out later it's barely C-level.

Sadly, I didn't learn this lesson until graduate school: Some professors were willing to review 20-plus-page papers, but two things had to happen:

a) The papers had to be submitted two weeks before the actual due date; and

b) I had to tell the professor my intentions to submit the paper early.

How sad that during my undergraduate years I missed an important fact: When a goal involves an evaluation by another person, both parties should share an *early* discussion about what's required to meet that goal. Think of a football coach who doesn't talk about intended plays before practices or a major game, but instead only evaluates what players did wrong after a loss. Crazy, right? When you don't have an early conversation to tell your prof about your grade goals, you're setting yourself up for the real possibility that you won't meet those goals.

Ask Yourself This:

When have I planned for other goals and what were they? Trying out for a sport? Applying for a job I wanted? Saving for an item I wanted to buy?

Think of the process you laid to reach those goals. Reaching for academic goals requires the same mindful planning.

Also Ask Yourself:

When I had other goals, did I go to key people who could help me and ask questions? What questions did I ask? What questions do I now realize I should have asked?

Think This:

My prof is my partner in helping me reach my grade goals. If I don't start the discussion with my prof and start it early, I won't know how to maximize my shot at reaching my goals.

Not That:

It's too late to talk to my prof since I didn't do it at the beginning of the term.

Unless it's the second-to-last week of the term, talk to your prof anyway. Depending on when you initiate the conversation, there may be a lot or little you can do to bolster your final grade. However, if you don't start the discussion, you won't know if you can get what you want … or rescue your grade.

Say This:

On the first day or during the first week:

I'm trying to get into the nursing program, and I have a goal of getting a 3.5 in this class. Do you have any advice to make that happen? Can I submit work early? If so, how early would you like me to turn in my assignments so you'll have time to give me feedback, and so I can work on what you tell me to? Are you willing to look at my work again after I apply your recommended changes? When should I check back with you to make sure my goal is on track?

Not That:

In week 9 or 10:

But I needed a 4.0 in this class!

You should have thought ahead. Furthermore, if a professor is trying to help you reach your goal, never say, "That's too hard!" or "That's too much work!" Your credibility will be shot.

The End Note

I probably don't need to tell you this, but just discussing grade goals won't guarantee the grade you seek. You have to do the work, and your work must meet the requirements of the grade you want.

Telling your prof about your intentions sets the tone for a consistent feedback loop and you'll partner with your professor every step of the way. Best of all, you won't be blindsided by a grade.

You won't even need to resort to bribery.

Chapter 9

Passing a Course After Absences

What You Might Say:

Can I still pass this class?

What Your Professor Thinks:

You haven't shown up for three weeks. What do you suggest?

The Real Story

Madelyn attended class regularly until her work schedule changed. She didn't tell me about the change, but just stopped attending. I placed her in the "fell off the face of the earth" category. Then Madelyn got laid off from her job and turned up in class one day.

She asked, "Can I still pass?" despite missing three weeks.

Let's talk about another student, Parris—another steady attendee—until her mother was diagnosed with cancer. She had to take her mother to treatment, which conflicted with our class times. Parris anticipated she would miss at least four classes, possibly more. Parris had strong grades in all her classes. Although it would be understandable if she said, "Hey, I can't do school right now because of my Mom," she told me what was happening, and asked, "Is there any way I can stay in this class and finish the term?"

Parris was no longer as concerned about acing the class, but she wanted to finish. She might lose her financial aid funding if she didn't stay on track.

The Back Story

Life happens when you're in college. I know this because life happened to me in the same way. When I was 21, my father unexpectedly died. What did I do? I stopped going to class, even though only a few weeks remained in the term. I didn't talk to the professors to find out my options; I just faded away. Unfortunately, it took me six years to return to college. I didn't plan for *that* to happen, but I can relate when my students fall into a life situation and fall out of college.

What MIA (missing in action) students don't realize is their names still show up on my roster, which tells me they haven't dropped the class. I can't withdraw them, so if they don't drop, I have no choice but to give them a 0.0 grade. Essentially, an F.

This breaks my heart!

I hate to lose students under any circumstances. I tell students in my syllabus and on the first day that I'm capable of finding creative options to save a desperate situation—but only if I know about that situation as soon as it happens.

I am sensitive to life situations—big, small, and unexpected, like when my father died. I know many students in this day and age are maxed out, working one job or two while juggling family responsibilities, emotional challenges, and unexpected tragedies. College seems like the last thing on your mind when you're going through something difficult and can barely slog through another day.

But ask yourself this: "Am I prepared to drop this class before the required date to avoid an F on my transcript?"

If the answer is "no" or even "I don't have it in me to make that decision right now," then you owe it to yourself to contact your prof and find out if you can still finish the course. Your prof can help you with the decision.

Keep in mind that the responsibility is totally on *you* to reach your prof quickly, whether you've already missed class or you're going to miss class. Read the syllabus and check out the attendance policy before you step into your prof's office. Calculate worst and best-case scenarios based on the days you missed (or will miss) and see if you can stomach that grade outcome. Granted, your prof may give you a free pass and not penalize you, but you can't count on that. Become comfortable with the current policy and its ramifications, then feel relief if the prof offers you something else.

If you can deal with the grade outcome, your next step is to see *what* you've missed (or will miss), either by looking at the class schedule or talking to a classmate.

Keep in mind you are taking these actions *before going to see your prof.* You need to approach your prof with a strategy to offer, rather than asking her to create a plan for you.

Let me say that again: *You have a much better chance of saving the situation if you develop a proposal to show your prof, rather than expecting her to do reactive crisis management.*

When you do see your prof, what you choose to discuss about why you missed class is your choice. You don't have to share personal information. Honestly, the reasons why you were out don't matter.

I'm not saying your prof doesn't care about you. Most profs care about their students very much, but your prof is in problem-solving mode to get you through *now*. Mulling over the reasons you were out for three weeks isn't going to help determine if you can stay in class. You can mention the problem if you wish, but your time is better spent discussing your proposal, once you plan it.

For that important "save your ass in class" meeting with your prof, make an appointment and be up front about what the meeting is for: You've missed a quite a few classes and you want to discuss your options for staying in the course. You may decide during this meeting that you'd be better off dropping the class. If you want to take this prof's class again, however, he will already know you and have more respect for you if you initiate a conversation about your status instead of fading away.

Before I move on to your talking tips, let's tackle this from a different perspective: Some students who miss classes never plan to return. Believe it or not, a professor may actually attempt to contact *you* if he sees you started coming to class, but now you aren't. Don't expect this: Most profs won't because of a possible FERPA violation. (Under the FERPA law, a professor cannot ask or answer questions of anyone who may pick up your phone.)

If I'm trying to find out a student's status, I will often e-mail instead, because there's a better chance the student's eyes are the only ones on the account. If I'm certain I have a student's cell phone number, I may take that route.

Ask Yourself This:

Do you have a history of missing class and then scrambling to catch up? How does this make you feel? Stressed? Overwhelmed? If you're missing classes, what stops you from talking to your prof about your situation? Do you feel embarrassed? Worried? Scared?

Think This:

If a life situation happens to me, or I become so overwhelmed in a class that I want to stop going, the best thing I can do is talk to my prof immediately. I shouldn't make any decisions on my own without exploring my options. I can still decide not to stay in the class, but at least I'll either get the help I need or figure out whether I can handle the work that's left. The prof has dealt with these situations before and isn't there to judge me for missing class. The prof is there to help me figure this out.

Not That:

It won't matter if I talk to my prof or not. She doesn't want to help me because I've missed so much class.

If you're proactive about how you intend to save your term, your prof will hear you out and have more respect for you than if you ask her to solve the problem for you.

I can probably take the penalty and then catch up. My grade won't suffer.

Many students overestimate how well they can do after missing classes. You will have to bring yourself up to speed; your prof will not go over the material for you. Also, expect to face a penalty that's probably noted on your syllabus. Plan your possible points with that penalty included.

Say This:

The moment you know you'll have to miss a series of classes, say to your professor:

I'm going through something serious and unexpected right now. I'm going to miss some classes (say how many if you can), but I'm committed to finishing the course. I've looked ahead at the schedule and see you're covering X chapters. I believe I can work through those myself. I also realize there will be a penalty for my absences.

I've calculated that even if I score low points for the remaining assignments, I can still leave this class with a C. Am I taking everything into consideration, given my circumstances? Do you have further advice for me so I can get through this class?

Make sure you check in with your prof if your return is delayed. Continue letting him know how you plan to stay on top of your situation. Here's another option if you're early enough in the term:

Could I switch to another format of this class, such as online or hybrid?

I've seen students find relief from a rigorous in-class schedule when they move to an online or mostly online format. See if this will work for your situation.

If you haven't contacted your professor ahead of time and you've already missed a lot of class, say,

I missed a lot of class and it was unavoidable. I don't plan to miss any further classes, and I'm hoping to finish. I realize I should have gotten in touch with you much sooner. I know I'll probably end up with a lower grade than I originally wanted. I looked at the syllabus and see that I've missed X chapters. I will go over those myself. Will you accept some specific questions if I have them? Also, I reviewed the syllabus and see my absences will cost me X-number of points. If my calculations are correct, even with low grades on the remaining assignments, I can still get a C out of this class. Can you confirm that I'm looking at this situation correctly? Do you have other advice for me? I appreciate your willingness to work with me and I apologize for not getting in touch with you sooner.

Caution here: Your prof can't insist you drop the class, but she can tell you if your plan is missing something. This is when you have to decide whether you'll fight to stay in the class or consider taking it at another time.

Not That:

Can I still pass this class?

Acknowledge you've missed class before asking this—and figure out for yourself if you can still pass.

Or,

> Can you just not ding me for being absent?

The prof has to do that for every single student if he does it for you.

Or,

> I have a note proving I was in the hospital, or my grandmother was in the hospital partially eaten by wolves (just kidding).

Most college classes don't recognize excused versus unexcused absences. A missed class is a missed class. Every student faces challenges and the prof doesn't want to play judge and jury to determine if your ill aunt is more excusable than another person's doctor appointment. Therefore, unless your prof says she needs a note (the syllabus would mention this), don't bother mentioning it.

The End Note

I almost always try to save a student's term if it's humanly possible. From my own experience losing my dad, I know what an F does to a transcript. I know that unless you retake the class, that F will weigh down your GPA and hinder other academic opportunities.

Even though a C or D aren't grades you want to think about, you can at least pull your credit out of the course and average up your GPA with high grades in other courses. (Disclaimer: A "D" in some programs may not allow you to pull your credit out—check with your program to be sure). Sometimes dropping will be the only answer, but even withdrawal is better than failing.

It's easy for me to say, "Just go to class no matter what," but I didn't do that when my father died. I didn't talk to a prof either.

I hate to sound like a parent instead of a prof on this one, but take my advice and do better than I did. Go see your prof and try to work on your situation. I bet you'll figure something out.

Chapter 10

A Do-Over

What You Might Say:

Phew. Professor Hero is letting me redo that paper. I have more time.

What Your Professor Thinks:

A do-over is a gift, and requires an immediate thank-you by turning in the work quickly.

The Real Story

Liam turned in a speech via recording for my online class. In it, he read the entire presentation word-for-word. He had no eye contact with the camera, no interaction with the audience, and he used a monotone voice.

I contacted Liam and said, "I need to discuss something with you and it won't be easy to hear. It isn't easy to say either. I can't accept your speech because the whole thing was read. Your lack of eye contact and interaction with the audience means the speech didn't meet the minimum requirements for this assignment."

Liam nervously asked, "Will I get a zero?"

I replied, "Well, you should. But it's important to me that you learn to use speaker's notes. So, I'm going to have you redo the speech and take a late penalty. We'll probably both be a lot happier about your grade."

If you think I gave Liam a big break, and one that was unfair to the rest of the students who can't redo their speeches, I can see why you have that perception. But let me tell you, re-recording speeches in my online class is a complete and total pain in the ass. The student has to gather an audience all over again and deliver a speech they've already mentally (and, might I add, happily) put away.

I'll also tell you that for many profs, like myself, who have a syllabus statement warning, "Don't ask me to do something I can't do for everyone in the class," even with the greatest intentions of fairness, we take extreme student issues on a case-by-case basis and we lift our rules.

We allow the do-over.

So let's talk about how the do-over looks in a case like this: My expectation is that Liam will thank me for the opportunity to redo his speech, rather than take a zero, and he'll set a firm date with me to submit this assignment. The date will be within a reasonable timeframe, not weeks away. Liam will take it upon himself to check and see when the next assignments are due so he doesn't back himself up against those deadlines.

When Liam does submit his revised speech, he won't repeatedly ask me when I'll grade it. Instead, he'll review the policy in my syllabus that says, "Late work does not get priority grading over a) on-time work I'm reviewing before a major assignment, or b) major assignments already submitted on time." He will move swiftly to work on the next assignment and will definitely not repeat the same scripted delivery.

The Back Story

What I *want* to happen is different from what often *does* happen in the land of the do-over. Liam's scenario will play out in one of several ways:

1. The ideal: He'll set a date with me to submit the work and turn it in quickly.
2. The worst: Liam may not redo the work at all, and he'll end up with a zero grade.
3. The also-not-great: Liam may redo the work, but wait so long to submit that he can't possibly use the feedback to help him on the next assignment.

Sadly, most students fall into scenarios 2 and 3, making me feel like a moron for even offering the kindness of the do-over. On top of that, let's go back to the fairness issue: You can imagine the uproar when other students hear that someone who did poor work had a chance to revise his assignment and re-submit. They say, "Hey, I'll do crappy work the first time around too, and then I'll have extra days to get it right."

Do-overs aren't fun for anyone. Sure, there's the chance for a better grade, but who wants to do work a second time when other assignments loom ahead?

Profs are also negatively affected by do-overs. Think about it: In Liam's case, I already reviewed his recording. Then I agreed to review the same speech again, which means I spent more time on Liam than on any other student. And all this happened because he didn't get his speech right the first go-around and I allowed him a do-over.

You know as well as I do that it feels good to have a stack of work completed. When I have a bunch of grading to do, I set aside a number of hours, get into the mindset of that assignment's requirements, and then dive in and get a rhythm going. When Liam turns in his new speech, this might be when I'm doing early review of students' work for the next speech, or, worse, when I'm already grading recordings for the next speech. I'm already in a totally different place. Consider being super-focused on an English lit paper, and then someone says, "Hey, time to shift to algebra now!" You can switch gears, but you have to get into a different mindset.

Sure, when I allow a do-over, I accept the consequences of that decision. I just want you to realize that sacrifice is involved for your professor. This is why not turning in the work at all, waiting a long time to turn it in, or pestering your prof about the grade are huge offenses.

Let's start with not turning the work in at all. Remember what I said about any points being better than a zero? This is not a gift you want to ignore. If you wait to turn the work in, there's a good chance you'll never get around to it—or the quality may suffer because you've already moved on to other things. Also, you aren't giving your prof time to offer feedback that will boost your next assignment (which I know you will pay extra-special attention to because of your do-over gift, right? You = "Yes!").

Finally, please do not bug your prof to grade the assignment. Your prof cannot put your redone work before other work that was submitted on time—that would be *very* unfair to your fellow students. And, she has no obligation to give you substantial feedback or a definite timeframe for returning your work. Sure, it would be nice if you received your grade and the feedback right away, especially if your redone assignment could help you with other work. But you have no guarantees this will happen. Submit the redone work quickly and know your prof wants to get this extra grading done as much as you want the grade.

Ask Yourself This:

What prevented me from doing the work right the first time? Did I understand what was required? Did I need additional help? Am I willing to get help next time, rather than spend extra time redoing my work?

Think This:

Redoing work means more time and more work. I'm better off making sure I know exactly what to do the first time and trying to do my best.

Not That:

It doesn't matter how I do on this assignment. I can either redo it or take a zero.

Your prof may not allow a redo and a zero will damage your overall grade.

Say This:

If a redo isn't offered to you, say,

I realize I didn't do my best on the first attempt for this assignment. I believe I can do better. Is there any way I can redo it for partial credit?

If your professor agrees, then say,

When would you like me to resubmit my work? Can you give me an idea of how the points will work since it's a redo?

You might go on to say,

I realize that, of course, you will be grading other assignments first, but can I expect to use the feedback from this assignment for the next one?

If your professor says no, then don't push it. Instead, you can say,

I want to make sure I don't make this mistake again. When should I meet with you to get help for the next assignment and make sure I'm on track? Will you review that work early for me? How will this grade affect my overall grade?

Not That:

> You have to give me another chance!
> This isn't fair! I didn't understand what I was supposed to do! I know
> I can do better next time!

If your prof doesn't allow a do-over, he has a good reason. Nothing you say will change his mind, so move forward to the next assignment and try to strengthen your grades as much as possible.

The End Note

Based on my thoughts in this chapter, you may be surprised to hear that I actually believe heavily in do-overs, also known as mastery learning (basically, doing a task until you master it). We adults learn through repetition and the most effective learning occurs through a cycle of feedback and revision. I've actually been known to let an entire class redo an assignment if I felt it would help them.

In fact, if I had my way, I'd authorize do-overs all the time, because my students would get a ton of practice in interpersonal communication and public speaking. That would be a dream come true for me.

But I don't have my way. College terms have to end.

While doing work over again may mean a better grade for you, it also has negatives: If we know we can redo something, we don't go all out on the first try. In the real world, do-overs aren't always possible—our first attempt has to be our best attempt. Also, redoing work means extra effort when a little additional time and care on the first pass could save hours of revision.

A redo is a gift. Don't take it for granted—it's a big deal. Turn in your do-over quickly. Use the opportunity to make the rest of your assignments even better.

That's the best thank-you card you can offer your prof.

Chapter 11

Extra Credit

What You Might Say:

My grade is too low. Can I do some extra credit?

What Your Professor Thinks:

Extra credit can't save a failed quarter.

The Real Story

Angelo missed a required journal assignment worth 100 points. He was concerned about his overall grade and asked, "Can I do some extra credit to make up for this?"

Few professors would offer 100 points of extra credit. Five points, 25 points, maybe 50 points, but 100 points? Not likely.

Let's say I give Angelo extra credit worth 20 points (that would be about my average). He'll need time to do the extra credit work in addition to the next assignments in my course. Sure, Angelo technically saved time because he didn't do his journal assignment (though that time is already gone, right?). But now he must finish not only the required upcoming work, but also an additional assignment. Angelo would have been better off—time-wise and points-wise—turning in only part of the journal assignment. Even a failing grade would come out to 50 points, which is more than he'll earn with extra credit.

Here's another example: Marjorie received a C on one of her speeches because the lack of quality sources lowered her grade. Like Angelo,

Marjorie wants extra credit to move her C closer to a B. Instead of Marjorie putting all of her time and attention into finding excellent sources for her next speech (due in three weeks), she'll need to work on that speech *and* do my extra credit assignment.

Marjorie *could* have saved time by kicking butt on the points-bearing work and getting a high grade, rather than tasking herself with extra work.

Let's look at one final student: Tyler, a strong student who has an A and doesn't even *need* extra credit, but wants it as an insurance policy. If Tyler does extra credit, he'll take energy away from A-level work required for my class … or another class. Is that extra credit really worth it?

The Back Story

I know this is an unpopular thing to say, but extra credit is *so* not worth it!

Many students who pursue these points don't actually need them, and the rest would benefit more by focusing on the work they have to do anyway.

Let's start with students like Tyler, who don't need the extra credit, but want it for insurance. I often dissuade these students from extra credit by saying, "Your points are already high. Why don't we wait a little while and see if you actually *need* the extra credit." On nearly every occasion with high-achieving students, their A is secure.

So let's focus on everyone else: In my course (and many courses like mine), profs use a variety of tools to gauge student knowledge and ultimately come up with a grade, including writing assignments, public speaking, quizzes, and tests.

If your prof offers early review of work, then you have a great opportunity to let your prof evaluate your assignment, give you feedback, and then you can fine-tune. Doesn't this make more sense than doing sub-par work and then taking more time to do extra credit? Even studying three times as long for an exam makes more sense than starting all over on a new extra credit assignment that may not even give you enough points to help.

I will make one exception to the concept of no extra credit. If you're taking a class where your entire grade hinges on a series of examinations and quizzes and there's *no* other way to show what you know, then you may need to request extra credit. We all understand that not everyone tests well. An exam is a snapshot of someone's knowledge at a single moment of time, rather than an ongoing work in progress like a research paper, a speech, or even homework consisting of mathematical equations.

Without getting into a lot of boring learning theory, having a grade built solely on quizzes and examinations can be problematic for a student. A student should receive a grade based on different ways of showing knowledge, but not every professor feels that way. If you happen upon one of these professors and your tests aren't going well, this *is* one time that you may need to ask for extra credit.

The extra credit could take the form of going back to your incorrect test questions and writing a brief explanation of why you missed those items and what you now know about them. This will require more work and research on your part, but guess what? You will actually KNOW the material, which should be your professor's goal, rather than the pump and dump method (pump yourself full of the information necessary to do well on the test and then mentally dump that information shortly thereafter).

I'm not saying your professor will even offer extra credit in a situation like this, but you certainly could ask. This will go over far better than telling your prof that his entire means of measuring your knowledge is flawed. Giving you a bit of extra credit is easier for a professor then revamping an entire curriculum he may have used for years.

One note of caution: If you do ask for extra credit, make sure it will actually help your knowledge and overall grade. The extra credit will be a huge time-waster if you don't learn anything, or if the few points you earn don't help your grade.

Ask Yourself This:

Do I often rely on extra credit to bring my grades up? Do I ask for extra credit a lot? What prevents me from achieving the strongest grades on regular classwork? Am I devoting enough time to that work? Do I need additional help? Am I asking for my work to be reviewed early? Am I asking enough questions?

Think This:

Extra credit won't be needed if I do the absolute best job I can on the work I have to do. If I do need extra credit and my prof offers the opportunity, at least I'll know I did everything I could and it's worth spending my time on a few extra points.

Not That:

I don't have to do well on this assignment. I'll just ask for extra credit to bring my grade up.

Remember, not every professor offers extra credit. A little extra credit isn't going to make a substantial difference, and you'll be taking time away from assignments that are still due, or work in other classes. Also, only a ton of extra credit will save an entire term's poor grades, and I don't know any professors who would let you do enough extra credit to raise your grade a significant degree.

Say This:

I was looking over my grade and see I'm close to getting an A (or whatever your next grade threshold is). I'd really like to make that happen. Do you have some advice about the assignments that are still due so I can earn as many points as possible? Will you take a look at some of my work early? When should I get that to you?

If you're hell-bent on doing extra credit, but there are more assignments to come, say:

My grade isn't quite where I was hoping it would be. I'm wondering if extra credit is available. I'd be glad to either take a second look at the work I've already done or do an additional assignment. I'll be sure to work harder on the next assignments coming up. Would you be willing to review them ahead of time?

If nothing else is due for class and your overall grade is low, say,

I realize I should have done things differently this term. I have a much lower grade than I was hoping. I'd like to bring it up, even a little bit. Do you offer extra credit and would it help my average?

If your class falls into the scenario I mentioned above where your entire grade hinges on quizzes and exams, say,

I didn't do well on my quizzes/exams and my grade is low. I'm concerned about that and also believe I know more about this material than the test scores show. Is there anything I can do to raise this grade?

In this scenario you aren't directly asking for extra credit, but if your prof offers you an option to raise the grade, extra credit is essentially what you'll be getting. If possible, show your prof any homework or other lesser assignments to back you up.

Not That:

Why can't I just do extra credit to bring up my grade?

Extra credit is a privilege and a benefit; your prof is never obligated or required to offer it. Your prof *is* obligated to help you do your best on the required assignments as long as you're working hard on them.

End Note

Rethink your perception of extra credit. One of my favorite college/high school success authors and popular Study Hacks blogger, Cal Newport, has a mantra: "Work smarter, not harder."

Remember this when you consider tapping into extra credit to raise your grade. Sure, those additional points *could* help you, but the time and the effort will take something away. Wouldn't you rather have time to work on another class, see a movie, or lie on your bed counting indentations in your ceiling?

Be selfish. Get the most out of what you have to do, and then you won't need to do extra.

Chapter 12

Finding Out What's On the Test

What You Might Say:
Will this be on the test?"

What Your Professor Thinks:
So the rest of the content isn't important?

The Real Story

I do a crazy class activity with my students involving distance. Students pair up and then we usually go outside into a courtyard if the weather is decent. I have the students walk about eight to 10 feet away from each other and try to carry on a conversation.

Then, the students step in closer where they can barely touch fingertips and continue their conversation. Next, students move where they can reach each other's shoulders, and the conversation goes on. (As you can imagine, things become a little uncomfortable at this point. But, just wait…).

Finally, students go toe-to-toe and attempt to carry on their conversation. Yes, they bend and twist, trying to avoid eye contact, and each other's coffee/pizza/morning breath. What the students are doing isn't quite as important as what they typically ask during this activity, and so many others: **"Will this be on the test?"**

I don't play these silly games for fun, even though most of them *are* fun (and this one is particularly enjoyable for me to watch—kidding!).

But there is an intentional lesson in everything I do: In this game, we analyze how people react nonverbally to Edward T. Hall's theory of proxemics. And, yes, Edward T. Hall's theory of proxemics *is* on a test.

I worry that students miss much of the actual experience because they're so busy worrying if what they're learning is worth paying attention to. You know—if it's test-worthy. Students spend too much of their college education wondering what's going to be on the next test. I believe it is one of life's biggest, most unanswered questions.

The Back Story

And one of life's biggest, pain-in-the-ass questions for professors! (Just saying!)

I don't want to get into a bunch of philosophy about how professors wish you would love learning for the sake of learning. How we wish you could just not worry about what's going to be on the test, because that tells us that you view everything else as throw-away knowledge.

How we'd love for you to absorb everything we're teaching you and believe that most of it will make you more worldly, more knowing, more, well ... educated ... all tests aside.

I know that just isn't reality.

Professors realize students are in school because, sure, they want to become smarter, more competitive, and many career paths require a college degree. To get the degree, you have to get grades. We *all* know that. Of course, you want to pinpoint *the exact material* to focus on so you can study your little heart out and ace your tests.

The problem is, many profs simply won't feed you the information that way.

Think about it: What would you be gaining in college if the prof walked in and told you, "Okay, write down pages 22, 25, 46, 53, 63, 77, 79-84, 90, 92, 94-98, and 102. That will all be on your next exam."

What would be the point of even coming to class? What would be the point of your entire college education? I mean, let's get philosophical for just one second. How would you be learning or expanding yourself? Isn't that what you're really in college for? To expand yourself? (And I'm not talking about the freshman 15).

I know a part of you agrees with me, even just a little. So does learning or expanding your mind mean that your tests should be a guessing game? No way ... and I'll actually discuss that topic later on in this book.

You shouldn't have to aimlessly study for your exams either, hoping to land on the right content. That's why we have course objectives. What you are tested on *should* relate to the course objectives listed in your syllabus. If you take those course objectives a little further and look at your weekly units or modules (depending on how your course is set up … chapters, folders, etc.), you may even see other objectives there.

All of those objectives give you a hint of what you'll probably find in the tests. If you see words like "demonstrate" or "explain" or "apply", those objectives mean you are going to *do something* with that information. So, you can probably guess the concepts within that objective will appear on some sort of assignment or test.

Let me give you a quick example: One of the major course objectives for my Intro to Communication course is: "Apply principles of cultural diversity to human/interpersonal communication, small group communication, and public speaking."

You see the term *apply*, right? This means students have to **show** they can do something. Translation: Some aspect of cultural diversity will be found on an assignment, and even more likely, on a test.

In my department, we cover cultural diversity concepts in our departmental exam, and we also look for intercultural competence in small group interactions, interpersonal writings, and in speeches. Now, you may be asking yourself, "Why do I have to be some academic brain surgeon when I can just ask my prof if that day's lesson is going to be on the test? Heck, I can ask my prof if that last sentence he said is going to be on the test."

You do *not* have to be an academic brain surgeon, but I recommend that during class time or while studying, notice when something matches up to some of the course objectives (or the module objectives). Then, you'll know if you should begin creating your own study guide for an upcoming test.

(Yes! You can create your own early study guide as you go, and then combine it with what you get from the professor, which I'll discuss in a second. Look how far ahead of the game you'll be!)

We can't forget that in all likelihood your prof *will* provide study guides, review sheets, and other items to help you prep for major exams. The goal is for you to be present when those documents are handed out, use them to study, and study them often.

If your professor hasn't provided a study guide, ask for one, or create one yourself. I'm going to recommend you do both, actually.

Ask Yourself This:

What do I expect to gain from my classes? Do I believe they're all about trying to pass tests? Or do I view my classes as a way to broaden myself as a person on the way to getting my degree?

When I ask my professor if something will be on a test, what do I expect her to say? Do I think she'll tell me every single answer in advance?

Do I believe I shouldn't have to study material that isn't on the test?

Am I worried I'll accidently learn something that won't be on the test?"

Am I worried I'll be wasting my time? Am I concerned that I'll fail if I don't study the right content?

Think This:

I'll probably find out what's going to be on my tests because the prof will offer study guides or do a review in class. I don't need to ask over and over again if a certain day's lesson is going to be on the exam. If I am worried about studying the wrong information, there are other ways to find out.

Not That:

I don't want to do a lot of extra work. I just want to be ready for the test.

As I pointed out, without the professor feeding you the answers, you're going to get what seems like extra learning. But in your professor's mind, there's nothing extra about it. Consider the title of your class. You have 10 to 15 weeks in a term. In that time, you will receive foundational, intermediate, or advanced instruction on a specific topic. And, you'll be tested. The tests are a by-product of learning. They may seem like the main event because they're tied to your grades, but in truth they are only one aspect of a greater learning picture.

Say This:

If your professor hasn't given any sort of study guide for major exams, say this at least two to three weeks before the exam (preferably, at the beginning of the term):

Professor, I see we have a couple of major tests coming up. I'll be working on my own study guides, but I'm also wondering if you'll be giving us a study guide or offering a review session in class?

If you're still afraid you aren't studying the right material, or wondering if certain content will appear on the test, here's the best way to inquire about it:

Have your professor's study guide in hand (if he gave you one). This document should have some of your own notes on the side and you should have a personal study guide you created (essentially, to show that you've done *something* yourself). This document could be mapped with the objectives I told you about earlier.

Then go to your prof and say,

Professor, I've been studying this for the exam and want to be sure I'm focusing on the right concepts. I made my own notes and even looked at some of the objectives to see what I should know at this point. Can you check my list of topics and make sure I'm reviewing the right information? I'd like to do as well as I can on this test. I'm trying to ace it, if possible.

Just the idea that you would,

a) create your own study guide; and

b) use the objectives and try to do something with them is going to spin your prof's head around—in a good way.

Not That:

You know that lesson you did yesterday? Is any of that going to be on the test? What about the day before? How about what we're doing tomorrow?

Your prof is going to know you just want to be fed answers and you aren't interested in learning the material. Even if you actually are interested, your message isn't going to come across that way. Get the answers that you really need by showing you've taken action to help yourself first.

The End Note

I don't discuss communication and your overall image a lot in this book, but I'm sure you've realized by now that my underlying message is this: *I want you to sound smarter and less clueless.* I *know* in my heart that students just do not realize how grating it is when they ask what content will be on a test.

I'll put it in this perspective: What if you went into work every single day and asked your boss, "Will doing this task get me a raise?"

You wouldn't do that, would you?

No!

You'd do an excellent job, show your boss what you can do, and then wait for review time to ask questions about how you're doing and what kind of raise you might expect.

Over and over again in this book, you will hear me say that you'll get much more help and respect from your professors if you do some work first, then approach them armed with a plan, a proposal, or an attempt.

Then, your words will mean so much more—even if you're trying to get a clue about what's on an upcoming test.

Chapter 13

Your Work Ethic

What You Might Think:

Work ethic? That doesn't matter so much in college because I'm not getting paid.

What Your Professor Thinks:

Your work ethic in college is your work ethic in life. The environment doesn't matter.

The Real Story

Every prof can recall certain conversations with students that we know will stay with us for years. For me, one of these conversations was with Trent, an advisee, and also a student who'd taken a number of classes with me. Trent seemed absolutely fine with mediocre work, though I knew he was capable of so much more.

Trent was totally getting what we did in class. When we talked about using the assertive message in Intro to Comm, Trent said, "Wow, I used that last night with my brother, and I couldn't believe what a difference it made." He even gave a quick example.

During my Interpersonal Comm class, where we discuss family, professional, and romantic relationships, Trent told me what he learned changed his life. He was using the communication strategies almost daily to strengthen his relationship with a new girlfriend.

If you're thinking Trent was sucking up, believe me, his grades didn't reflect it. Trent failed to apply what he knew to his actual assignments. His work was often late and the quality was just not there.

One day, I decided to have a heart-to-heart with Trent. I said, "What's up? You clearly know this material, but I'm not seeing that in your work. I'd love to see you get the grades you deserve, based on your knowledge. You know a lot about communication!"

Trent shocked me with his reply. With a straight face, but a relaxed smile, he said, "I just don't need to stress in school. I've never been a good student anyway."

Confused, I said, "Well, isn't this the time to change all that? What you did in high school doesn't matter now. College is the place to build your work ethic."

"I will," Trent said, "when I go to work."

"When you go to work?" I asked.

"Yeah," Trent said, "when I get paid money, I'll do better."

Fortunately, most students do not share Trent's perceptions about building a work ethic in college.

Take Allie. She was one of my highest achieving students—a high school student taking college classes. She was constantly in my office checking on her grades and making sure she was on the right track. Allie was also heavily involved in campus activities; she was a leader of several clubs and part of the Honor society. Allie was going to graduate with her high school diploma and her first two years of college completed simultaneously. Not easy!

I remember talking to Allie about how she juggled it all. I knew her parents worked varied shifts and sometimes she had to care for her siblings. Allie simply said, "I have to do this, because it will change my life."

Allie had a fire in her. Coasting was not in her vocabulary. She was hell-bent to build a work ethic that will always be part of her life.

The Back Story

I believe some students think their work ethic will fall into place once they become paid employees. My take on that? (Because you want to know, right?) Who you are in this moment is who you are. If your work ethic is crap right now, then that *is* your work ethic. Own it and be loud and proud, or strive to change it. But don't fool yourself into believing you will miraculously behave differently once a job is in front of you.

Sure, we put on different faces with our friends and families. I don't deny that. But our motivation, drive for excellence, reliability, and commitment to a task well-done are all based on habit and past experience. For some of you, college is the first place where you're held accountable for the quality of your work. We could say you're being paid for that work with a grade. I know it's sometimes hard to look at grades this way. Grades don't feel tangible, but the workload leading up to them sure as hell does. The way you approach that workload says a ton about you.

Do you tackle your work head-on? Or do you slack and make excuses? If it's the latter, then someday when you actually face a task you don't like at your real job, you may slack there, too. Will a paycheck change poor work habits like procrastination, lack of attention to detail, unreliability, or absence of motivation? Maybe, but the changes probably won't be immediate, and look at the benefits of good performance you missed in college.

Ask Yourself This:

Do I believe college doesn't matter because my grades won't make a difference in what I eventually want to do with my life? What words would I use to describe my work ethic right now? Am I happy with my work ethic?

Think This:

The work I do in college can make a big difference for me when it's time to find a job. This isn't just about my grades, but about my work style. If I show commitment to and perseverance for hard work now, I'll be able to give examples of these situations during job interviews. I will also impress my professors, who may support me with recommendation letters or referrals.

Not That:

I'll figure out what type of work ethic I have when I need to worry about that. College is for having fun. I don't have to get serious about work just yet.

Wrong.

College is prime time to get serious about work—and having fun.

Say This:

May I submit work for early review?

Will you give me some help? I'm not sure I understand the concepts.

I want to do well in this class and have a goal of getting a 3.5. Can you make any recommendations for me?

I wonder if you can give me feedback on this paper? I started on it early so I could show it to you.

These are all phrases from students who have a high work ethic.

Not That:

I didn't get my paper done. Can I turn it in late?

Why did you give me a C grade? I thought I did better than that.

I missed the last two weeks. Can I still pass this class?

Ugh. What you're telling me to do requires too much work. Can't we make this easier?

I don't have to tell you what these phrases represent, do I?

The End Note

You are the only person who defines your work ethic.

Trent defined his: He was comfortable with a mediocre performance. He enjoyed hanging out with his friends and having fun. He attended class regularly, but other than just showing up, his work was barely above the minimum requirements.

Trent did take a job at a local fast food restaurant while he was in college. By the time he finished his two-year degree, he moved into management. He also stayed with his girlfriend and things were looking serious, like engagement serious. Suddenly, it seemed Trent was no longer content with a work ethic that wasn't consistent with the new roles his life demanded.

I give Trent credit. He did a hard re-examination on himself and turned things around.

Be honest with yourself about the habits you're creating. These habits don't have to define you forever. At any point, you have the power to change what you're doing and the way you're doing it.

And here's the best part: Dozens of people in college—from your professors to the support staff—are waiting to help you.

Chapter 14

Asking for Help or a Review (Early!)

What You Might Say:

I couldn't understand the concepts, so I just didn't do the assignment and I didn't think I could ask for help.

Or:

Can you look over this paper for me? It's due tomorrow.

What Your Professor Thinks:

I sure wish I'd known you were confused. I could have brought you up to speed before the assignment was due. You're leaving me little time to look at this and leaving yourself less time to carry out my recommendations.

The Real Story

In week eight of a 10-week term, Ty e-mailed me about his grade: "I see my average is a D. Can you tell me what's up?"

My response:

"Well, I see you missed doing an annotated bibliography. That was worth 100 points. I also show several of your quizzes are incomplete."

From Ty:

"I didn't know how to do the annotated bibliography. That totally confused me. And I started the quizzes, but then my computer froze and I couldn't get back into them."

Now me:

"I wish I'd known you were confused about the annotated bib! I would have been glad to help you. If you had a technology problem with the quizzes, had I known about it when the issue happened, I could have reset them for you."

And back to Ty:

"I figured I'd just have to lose the points. Sorry about that."

Let me give you another example: Breanna wrote a research paper for my Interpersonal Class and actually submitted an early draft. Sadly, the paper was a mess! Her thesis didn't make sense, and from there the organization was so choppy I couldn't follow her line of reasoning.

I could sort of figure out the direction Breanna was going, so I made suggestions for a new approach. Breanna did get points for submitting her draft, but never turned in her final paper. Even worse, this particular class presents their papers in mini-round table conferences at a high school. Breanna showed up with a draft version of her paper in hand.

I took her aside and said, "Did I miss getting your final paper?"

"No," she replied, looking away.

"I can't have you do a presentation based on this paper, Breanna. It needed too much work."

She looked at me and huffed, "I didn't know what to do!"

Calmly, I responded, "I wrote out what you could do. I gave you options for a new thesis and even suggested some main points."

"I saw that. But I didn't understand."

"Why didn't you tell me so I could help you further?"

Breanna didn't respond. She just sighed. Sadly, I had to give her the choice to stay and listen to her classmates present their papers, or leave the high school, return to college, and meet with me at a separate time so we could figure out the next steps. Since the presentations in that class occur at the bitter end of the term, there wouldn't be many options. Depending on Breanna's grade on her other work, she would likely fail the course because her final paper and presentation were worth 350 out of 1000 possible points. If her work was solid, she *could* receive an incomplete, but that would be a huge stretch for a non-academic reason, and some colleges won't even allow it.

The Back Story

In the last chapter, I discussed work ethic, and in this chapter and the next two, you'll see examples of that work ethic. Asking for help is definitely a cousin of work ethic because getting assistance and securing resources when you don't know what to do can impact performance in such a huge way.

I wish I could understand why so many students perceive asking for help as a sign of weakness. Many students don't just fail to ask for help early—many won't ask for help at all. Let's look at the basic truths:

Professors got into the education business because they want to help students.

This is what we're paid for and what we voluntarily signed up to do.

Now let's talk about you: You signed up to be a student. You didn't come to college knowing most of the subjects you're studying. Who does, right? Therefore, you're expected to feel some confusion over the content, the structure of your class, and even policies. Really, if you think about it, it's your *job* to need help as much as it's your prof's *job* to provide it.

Shouldn't both of us do our jobs?

Let me give you a harsh reality: A professor's job doesn't include seeking you out and begging you to come for help.

The onus is always, always on you to ask for what you need.

I know students are often frustrated because a prof can't read their minds or somehow *know* they are struggling. The only way I ever know a student is having problems is when the student directly says he needs help with the work or the student earns a poor grade.

Let's focus on the poor grade for a minute: Sometimes I'll write on a student's paper, "Let's work together next time and try for a better outcome." How many of these students do you think ask me for help after I make the offer?

Not many.

I don't know how I can convince you to ask for help if you're hell-bent on not asking. But, if I've persuaded you in the least—and I hope I have (because it's both of our jobs, remember?), then the primary message in this chapter is to ask for the help early enough to reap the benefits.

Of the students who do seek assistance, too many wait until they no longer have time to take my advice and implement it in a thoughtful way. Although your prof can give you specific guidelines regarding how early you should be asking for help, the ideal time is the day you realize you're confused. Even if you've just been assigned a research paper or a page of calculus homework and class time has ended, it's never too early to ask questions even if you *think* you only have a partial clue about what's going on.

After you've asked for general help with your work, then completed part of your assignment, I'm going to give you another major suggestion: *Ask for early review of your work, if your prof offers it.*

Some profs offer this service and others do not, but if your prof does it's like having him *bonus grade* your assignment without truly grading it. The benefit to you is that your prof will point out errors that would reduce the grade and give specific information about how to improve. If you take the recommendations, you know what *could* happen next: Your final grade may be better! Who wouldn't want that?

Of course, you *must* ask for the review early, and you must work early to get it.

Too many students don't take advantage of early review because they mistakenly believe their work is college-ready when it isn't, or they think their assignment is already perfect and doesn't need a pre-review. One poor grade sets them straight.

On the flip side, some profs won't offer early review because,

a) they believe students won't put their best effort into the first attempt (it's a valid concern, don't you think?), or

b) they don't think students will take the suggestions anyway, and then their own time will be wasted.

Let me tackle your perceptions about having perfect work on your initial try: In 14 years of teaching, I've *never* returned a review draft without giving feedback. Even if the outline or writing assignment is A-worthy, the student can almost always do *something* to improve. My goal isn't to make the student work like a circus animal, but to reach a new level of excellence. This is communication, after all, and that's my job: To help the student strive for more. I want to give my students every opportunity to feel articulate and confident.

Now let's take your prof's point of view: You perceive your time as valuable, and your prof feels the same way about his time. There's nothing worse than devoting an afternoon to reviewing work, then finding out that the student didn't take the advice given and the grade was no better.

My advice to you may seem obvious: If your prof does offer a review window, then take it! But honor the time window, and make sure you use the tips to improve your product.

With respect to honoring the time window, I can't tell you how many students abuse limits there. I always establish a Friday noon deadline for reviewing outlines or papers. This way, I know I can spend the entire rest of the day and evening looking at student drafts, and then the student has all weekend to do the work. I have two small children who are noisy and busy. My ability to look at an outline on a weekend is almost nonexistent because my only alone time is when I'm in the bathroom (and my laptop just does not belong there). You can't imagine how many e-mails I receive on Friday night or even Saturday morning begging, "Please, will you still review?" Or I get an email with no note, just an attachment, with the presumption that I will still take a look. Often, I send the documents back with a note saying, "We're outside of my review window. I'm sorry."

Know that if your professor sets time limits as I do, they are also for your benefit: You need adequate time to put feedback into place. In my class, a student working on a speech outline needs to make both outline changes *and* practice the speech. That takes time. And what if you're doing group work? Letting all group members fix their pieces of the project *really* takes time!

Ask Yourself This:

Do I feel ashamed about asking for help? What do I believe asking for help says about me? That I'm stupid? A failure? Have I felt bad about asking for help in other situations? What do I usually do instead? What negative consequences have I faced because I waited too long to ask for help? Have I ever had a positive experience asking for help? How did I feel when I received the help and was able to put it into place? Did I feel pride? Smart? Satisfied with myself?

What benefits will I gain if I work on a difficult assignment early and ask for review? Have I ever asked someone to review my work ahead of time and the feedback made my product better? How did I feel when that happened?

Think This:

I'm putting myself and my prof at a big disadvantage when I fail to ask for help. I'll stay confused and my grades could suffer. Or, if I wait too long to ask for help, I may not have time to put what I learn into place. If I work early on my assignment, my prof might even be willing to review it. If I need to make changes, I'll still be able to turn in the assignment when it's due. If I need more help, I'll have time to ask for it. My grade will probably be a lot better because I had the professor look at my work in advance.

Not That:

I don't really need any help. I'll figure this out on my own.

This only works if you have a good handle on what you're doing to begin with.

The prof is obligated to help me, so it doesn't matter when I ask.

Sure, the professor is obligated to help you, but we have limits. Any prof is well within her rights to say, "I've reached the point where I can't give you feedback you can use unless you plan to turn this assignment in late."

Just a note: This statement does not mean you're getting permission to turn in late work.

The prof is probably going to say my work is great. I doubt I'll need to change much, so I can wait a little longer.

The prof will review my work whenever I send it over. If there are changes, it won't take me long to take care of them.

For the first pass, it's best to assume you'll have plenty of work to do. If that isn't the case, you'll be pleasantly surprised. If you want a lot of time and less stress, get started and submit early.

Say This:

First, see when your assignment is due. Then, go to your prof and say,

I think I'm going to need help on this.

Other ways to say it:

I don't know what the heck is going on here and I need to figure it out.

Or,

I'm totally lost and would like not to be.

Don't want to give away how confused you are? Take a more subtle approach:

I think I have an idea what we're supposed to be doing, but just want to ensure I'm correct.

Or,

I'm unclear on this particular concept and I think I know why.

If you want to find out about a review, say,

Do you offer early review of my work if I'm willing to finish it early? How early should I plan to get it done so you have enough time to give me feedback?

If your prof agrees to review your work, say,

> Thank you very much. I'll be sure to have my paper to you by Friday. If I have questions after your review, should I e-mail those? Would you be willing to look at the paper again after I make the changes you've suggested?

If your prof has a policy that she won't review work in advance, then say,

> I realize you have a policy not to review work ahead of time. Would you be willing to look at one section of my paper and tell me if I'm on the right track? Can I send you specific questions about it?

Not That:

Saying nothing about your need for help is the worst thing you can do. Other statements to avoid:

> You didn't help me and that's why I didn't do well on this assignment.

If you didn't get the help you needed, blame isn't going to get you anywhere. Figure out why you didn't receive help. Did you try to ask for assistance and your professor was unclear? If so, you need to tell him,

> I'm sorry, but I'm not following what you're telling me.

Then reiterate the areas you do understand and ask the prof to rephrase or re-explain the information:

> I get what I'm supposed to be doing up through step five, but I'm completely confused after that point. I'm sorry to make you cover this again, but I want to make sure I truly understand.

Not That:

> I didn't feel like I should ask for help.

There is never a reason to avoid asking for help unless you're making the request the day the assignment is due.

> I just didn't know what to do.

Whenever a student says this to me, my next statement is always,

> Well, the first step would have been asking for help.

Regarding review work, if your prof does review ahead of time and you don't heed the deadline, saying nothing in an e-mail and attaching a file sends a message that you disrespect the prof's time. Don't do this.

Other statements to avoid:

> Will you still review this paper? I'm sorry I couldn't get it to you sooner.

If you're past the prof's window to review, then you've missed the opportunity. You can risk it and ask, and your prof may review, but the likelihood is she won't.

> But I wasn't expecting to do this much!

I will make a pointed statement here: If your professor cares enough to take extra time and give you feedback (because it's double the time on his part), don't complain about the amount of feedback. If your prof didn't give a rip about your grade, he wouldn't spend time trying to help you improve. I always tell my students, "I can handle your temporary anger if it means you're going to have a better outcome."

So, swallow your frustration and embarrassment. I know it isn't easy to take constructive criticism, but say thank you (not through gritted teeth), and then do your best to implement your prof's suggestions.

The End Note

I teach my public speaking students that when they verbally cite credible sources in their speeches, they should picture themselves carrying the experts from those sources piggyback in a "credibility totem pole." This is your mental image you should use when you use the "smarts" of your professors for extra support. Asking for help means you carry your prof's knowledge and wisdom on your shoulders.

To take this idea one step further, don't employers look for people who are resourceful? As an employee, you may not always have the right answers, but if you aren't afraid to ask the right questions you can figure out the answer.

College is the place to learn how to ask the right questions and to ask for help when you can't find the answers. So, when you need help, ask. And do it **early!**

Like right now! What are you waiting for? The answers are waiting— and so are your higher grades.

Chapter 15

Procrastination

What You Might Say:

I had a flat tire, a broken keyboard, or a hangnail that kept me from getting my assignment in by midnight.

What Your Professor Thinks:

Your lack of planning is not my emergency.

The Real Story

Avery e-mailed me hours before our assignment was due, saying, "Can you explain the citation requirements?"

Julian called me an hour before class and said, "My printer broke and I can't get my speech notes for my presentation tonight."

Marquez e-mailed me four times to say, "I tried to log on to the discussion forum to answer the questions before midnight, but my Internet isn't working!"

Let's take a closer look at each student's situation:

First, Avery: She needs me to explain the citation requirements for an assignment that's due in only a few hours. This is not a brief discussion. Just mention the word *citation* and you've opened a topic on which I cannot give a quick lesson. Also, I know a ton of work is required to find good sources for a presentation, not to mention incorporating those sources into the content, then practicing the newly included material. How is that possible in a few hours? It isn't.

Now, Julian: What's he going to do without speech notes? Can he still do his speech and wing it? (Not recommended.) Or will he decide not to show up? (Ugh! *Really* not recommended.) He knows our class meets only one night per week, so there's no time for a redo. I can't even imagine the stress Julian must be going through, knowing he has nothing to use at the podium.

And, finally, Marquez. Marquez doesn't realize that even if his Internet worked, students often wait until right before the midnight deadline to respond to discussion forum posts. In fact, one time the volume of students who logged on at the last minute imploded the server or the course management system (I was never sure which one, but let's just say the students couldn't get their work in).

Now, contrast those students with two others: Nelson was a student who admitted he received C's in high school because he didn't apply himself, although he was a solid writer. However, after one bad term in college, he decided to do better. Nelson finished his assignments early, which gave him the opportunity to check his work with me, and then follow up on my recommended changes. Nelson could have waited until the last minute to do his work, relying on his strength in the subject matter, but his grades were higher because he didn't.

Meghan was another student who worked early because she was the opposite of Nelson: Writing was a total struggle for her. Meghan knew she needed a lot of time to craft her outlines, and then even more time to implement the suggestions I inevitably made. Sometimes Meghan asked for a second pass on parts of her work. You can imagine how early she had to start to make this happen. I know my class wasn't her only one.

The Back Story

Do you detect a theme here? Students procrastinate—sometimes intentionally and sometimes unintentionally. I once saw a sign with the saying, "Your lack of planning is not my emergency." I should tattoo that statement on my forehead now that I teach college (don't worry … I won't).

Once again, my recommendation is going to seem like a no-brainer. You know I'm going to say, "Don't procrastinate! Plan your time better!"

But let's take a closer look at this issue, mainly, the stress on you. That's right: I want you to get selfish and realize how procrastination creates immense stress for *you*.

I know, you probably had a good reason for not finishing your work sooner. Maybe you were too busy, something unexpected came up, you had a true emergency, or you believed the work would be easy to tackle. What I bet you didn't plan for were the *other* things that could go wrong, like a computer crashing, Internet failure, a car breakdown, illness—I could go on and on. Bottom line: Aren't those risks more stressful than finding a way to work earlier so you aren't susceptible to unexpected issues?

Now let's focus on another source of stress. Suppose you wait until the last minute to ask for help on an assignment, like Avery with the citations. You get the answers, but you still need time to figure out how to implement them.

So, there you are: Still stuck with work that doesn't cut it. You will either have to submit the assignment as-is, fix it and take a late penalty (if that's possible), or not submit and accept a zero. Chances of getting an extension are slim. Don't you deserve to get the help you need early, so you can work in a more relaxed and informed manner from the start?

Finally, let's talk about how the professor views your procrastination. This may not cause you much worry, but it should. If you're asking questions at the last minute, or you have a sudden emergency that threatens your assignment, your prof is going to *know* you waited to start your work. This will *not* make you look credible.

Two chapters ago, we talked about college as a training ground to improve your work ethic and help you gain confidence through the excellence of your work. Procrastination is yet another example of work ethic.

You are the only person who knows your schedule and the obstacles you face in completing assignments. I am not unsympathetic toward what many of you juggle: families, financial issues, a job or two, or perhaps the stress of unemployment. Though you have other life challenges, it should come as no surprise that college work requires a lot of time—even if college constitutes your second or third job.

When you receive your syllabus during the first week of the term, your prof will likely give you a planned course schedule with due dates. Take a hard look at that schedule and consider *all* challenges you'll face for getting work accomplished, and accomplished well.

Try to estimate the preparation hours you need and whether those hours will include reading, researching, writing, revising, equating, or computing. Then, pull out your calendar and set personal work deadlines before the *actual* deadlines. A week ahead is ideal and two weeks is exceptional, but even a few days will give you time to deal with unexpected train wrecks.

I've said this often, but I'll say it again: Working early affords you a greater degree of help from your professor. I know this first-hand: When I was in graduate school, sometimes I had multiple 20-page papers due in one semester. I always knew if I completed the papers at least a week ahead of time I could show them to the professors and they would write comments in the margin. Had I waited longer, the professors wouldn't help me.

If you can't give yourself the time you need for small, minor projects, then by all means do so for large ones. Chances are, if these are high point-bearing assignments, you may need feedback from the professor not just once, but two or three times. Give yourself the best possible chance for success. You deserve it.

Ask Yourself This:

Do I procrastinate frequently? Why do I procrastinate? What stress do I experience when I put off work? What negative consequences have I experienced because of procrastination? Am I willing to continue accepting the downside of delaying my work until the last minute?

Think This:

I need to be honest with myself about my schedule and my habits. Procrastination is only going to cause me grief. Because I'll have to rush, I probably won't complete my work with the quality I'd like, and I won't have time to ask for help. I'm going to set a schedule for myself and reward myself when I meet those goals early. I may have to change things in my life, like getting together with friends and family, and maybe even my work schedule. But, I've chosen to be in school and my work—and my grades—deserve time and attention.

Not That:

I'll just wait to get this paper done. I'll have plenty of time a couple of days before.

What if you don't? Or,

Nothing bad has happened before when I've waited to work on my assignments. I should be fine.

What if you have an unexpected crisis or need more help than you realize?

Say This:

Tell a friend, family member, or even your professor:

> I'm trying not to wait until the last minute to complete my assignments. I realize I'm not allowing myself enough time and my work isn't as strong as I'd like it to be. Also, it's stressful. I'd like to check in with you to make sure I'm staying on schedule.

Anyone who cares about you (your prof included) will be supportive of your goal to change this part of yourself.

If you've procrastinated already and know you need help getting your schedule on track, tell your prof, "I have a bad habit of procrastinating. It has created a lot of stress for me and my grades have suffered. I'm going to make an effort to plan better. Can you work with me to figure out how early I should be working on my assignments? Can I check with you to make sure I'm on track?"

Not That:

> I didn't know what to do, so I didn't work on the assignment. What should I do now?

Your prof will wonder why you didn't ask for help sooner. Or,

> I forgot the assignment was due and just finished it. Can I have an extension?

Again, remember, your unintended delay will not trigger your prof to give you an extension. You will lose credibility if you tell your prof you couldn't keep track of the class schedule. Instead, make a decision to permanently change this habit.

The End Note

I know all too well that good planning is easy to talk about and hard to implement. My spouse went through an 11-month period of unemployment several years ago, and I had five grant/contract jobs going at once, as well as my full-time academic career. Add two small kids, and my schedule didn't seem to contain one spare minute.

Every single task required me to be at the top of my game. I couldn't miss class or not grade papers or I would disappoint students and risk losing my day job. I couldn't fall down on deadlines or I would risk not being hired again for well-paying grant/contract work, which would also hurt my professional reputation.

I followed my own advice, setting deadlines a week ahead of time for everything. I got up at 5 a.m. I worked well past midnight. I preferred to work longer days rather than let the projects slip closer to the deadline. I was exhausted, but I completed all my projects early—and kept my students satisfied. Everyone was happy.

I wasn't born with these habits. My mother will tell you I was a slob as a teen-ager, and to this day I can't keep house in a way that appeals to my husband. But I did develop critical habits in grad school when I had to turn in those complex papers I mentioned. Thank goodness, those habits stayed with me.

As you learn to prepare for and meet deadlines, you're building a work ethic just as I did. As we discussed earlier, if your work ethic isn't where you want it to be, college is the time to begin making small, positive changes to your habits. Without a doubt, this is one area you will not regret paying attention to.

Your stress level will thank you.

Chapter 16

Late Work

What You Might Say:

>   May I turn in this assignment late?

Or,

>   May I have an extension?

What Your Professor Thinks:

>   I can't give you permission without giving that same option to the 28 other people in the class.

The Real Story

Tanner misses an outline draft deadline. She catches me after class and says, "I was confused about the transitions, so I didn't turn in the outline."

Lladro sends me an e-mail: "My computer totally crashed and I lost my draft. Can I please have a three-day extension? I can't believe I have to start over again."

This is just a tiny sample of the widespread panic that occurs on assignment due dates. These students may or may not realize we are on the heels of another major assignment in two weeks (the quarter system moves fast!) and they risk a domino effect. One late assignment means less time to work on subsequent assignments—and then those may also be late.

The Back Story

I'm fairly certain "Can I leave early?" and "Can I turn in my work late?" are two of the most frequent questions profs get from students. They're also among the most frustrating statements students innocently make (I'll tackle "Can I leave early" in an upcoming chapter). Once again, turning in work late is another of those work ethic issues.

I discussed procrastination in the last chapter, and as you can imagine, late work often happens as a result. The student finds himself backed up against a deadline and realizes he can't get the work done; he experiences a "hit me on the side of the head like a train wreck" life emergency that prevents him from doing the work; or he's confused and doesn't ask for help soon enough.

These days, students rarely lie about dogs eating homework, grandmothers dying, and bulldozers smashing laptops (okay, I've never heard that one). You might think that's a good thing, but what's scary is the boldness replacing the lies. Many students will just casually shrug their shoulders and say, "Sorry ... didn't get to it."

Remember what I said about a work ethic in college reflecting your work ethic in life? This seeming lack of concern about late work as "just one of those things" scares me. Even worse, students have a sense of entitlement that profs should grant an extension without a second thought. Losing a few points is obviously no worry, or else the work would have been done on time in the first place, right?

The only real fear is if the professor simply accepts no late work under any circumstances. But many professors have some sort of late clause, and this may be unfortunate. I wonder if we educators are enabling poor work habits. We're almost giving students a choice: Submit on time to earn full points. Submit late and take a penalty, but not a major consequence.

I'm guilty of having a late policy that probably isn't strict enough. I will consider late work with penalty, but not after a new assignment period begins. In other words, in my theory class, a student can turn in the 100-point journal assignment during the period while we're still in that interpersonal communication section. Once we move on to constructing speeches, the time for submitting the previous assignment is over.

Let's shift to the confusion factor. If you didn't do an assignment because you're confused, your prof needs to know. I've discussed this in other chapters, so I won't repeat myself. But here are two key issues for you to consider:

First, when you turn in work late, you risk the domino effect of having other assignments end up late as well. What if the first late assignment takes more time than you expect, and it cuts into the time you need for your next assignment? See what I mean?

Next, a late assignment means that you probably won't get feedback early enough time to use for later assignments. So, you may get a grade, but nothing to help you for next time.

I *want* to tell you: "Never submit your work late!" But I know life sometimes gets in the way. What I want you to take away from this section is *do not ask for permission to be late with your work.* Just as your professor can't give you permission to leave class early and maintain fairness to the rest of the group, he can't offer you a free pass to turn in late assignments. So, don't ask, and don't make excuses about why you're late. Instead, create a *proposal* for your professor to consider—I'll explain that further below.

Ask Yourself This:

Do I have a habit of turning in late work? What's my usual reason for running late? Do I wait too long to get started? Am I unrealistic about how much time I need? How do I feel when I have to speak with a teacher about my late work? Do I feel embarrassed or ashamed? Do I feel nothing? What negative consequences have I faced because I turn in work late? What am I willing to do differently so I can keep this from happening?

Think This:

It's less stressful to plan in advance so I have plenty of time to finish my work and get help if I need it. I will feel proud of myself for working early and I'll be more relaxed about asking questions ahead of time. I'll probably be much happier with my grade because I won't be hit with a late penalty.

Not That:

Turning in late work doesn't matter. One late penalty won't hurt.

It might hurt a lot. What if your professor has a zero tolerance policy? Then, you'll have a zero. Or,

I'll have plenty of time to finish my other assignments, even if this one is late.

You can't know for certain how much time you'll need for future work, or what interruptions will occur in your life.

Say This:

Review the syllabus to see if your prof has a late policy, then say:

> Professor, my assignment's going to be late. This was unavoidable and I don't plan to make it a habit. I reviewed your late policy in the syllabus and I see I can turn in the assignment with a 50 percent penalty. I'll have the assignment to you in 48 hours. Will that be all right?

Realize you're probably relinquishing all rights to ask for help with the work—and particularly a review, but you can add,

> Are you able to answer questions if I have them, or has my time passed for that?

Another note here: Honor the date when you agree to turn in the work in. In fact, make absolutely certain you're prepared to meet that date before you even propose one. If you aren't sure how much time you'll need, ask the professor what she recommends—and find out if there's a variation in penalty:

> Professor, what's the latest date you'll be willing to accept this assignment? What penalty do I face if I have it ready in two weeks, rather than one?

If your professor doesn't have a late policy, you may be out of luck, but you can still ask,

> Professor, I'd like to complete this assignment. I realize you don't accept late work and I won't offer excuses to make you change your mind. But if I were to turn it in, could I receive *any* credit for it?"

If the prof agrees, then go back to the question about when to turn in the work.

Let's say you were totally confused about the assignment, which is why you didn't submit. This is something your prof needs to know, though she'll wonder why you didn't say something earlier.

Say,

> Professor, I realize I made a huge mistake not asking for help much sooner. I'm unable to turn in this assignment because I was confused about what we were supposed to do. I know I'm probably outside

my time to even ask for help, but I want to be successful next time. Would you be willing to help me get on track and let me submit the assignment? I won't let this happen again and I'll be sure to ask for help when I need it.

If your prof agrees, then she'll probably give you terms regarding when the material is due and your penalty. Alternatively, she may help get you up to speed in the class, but still won't let you submit the work. Be prepared that it could happen.

If you typically submit work on time and you *are* facing a life situation that makes your assignment late, say,

Professor, I'm usually right on time and even early with my assignments. I'm involved in a situation that's out of my control and I may have to be late with my next assignment. I read the syllabus and reviewed the late policy. I hope I don't need it, but I wanted to be prepared. May I show you the progress I've already made on my work?

Here you're being proactive, rather than forcing your prof to be reactive. You're taking responsibility for the possibility of late work, and in good faith you're showing the prof you've made a real effort already, consistent with your previous good habits. He may grant you more leniency, but don't abuse the generosity or lie to get more benefits.

One important note: Never, ever demand the prof grade your delayed work within a certain timeframe. My syllabus advises students I will never grade late work—regardless of the reason—before I grade current work or look at review work. That would not be fair to students who submitted on time.

Not That:

May I please have an extension for this assignment?

Your prof has to offer this to everyone if he offers it to you. Or,

I had a bad thing happen in my family and couldn't get my assignment done. I really need to turn it in late!

Don't offer excuses, because they just don't matter. Your professors do care about you, but they need to focus on action and solutions. So, your work is late. What the prof wants to know is, what do *you* intend to do about it now? Or,

It's not fair that you don't accept late work. What happened to me was terrible, or I would've had it done on time.

Life emergencies happen, sure. However, your prof anticipates you will schedule your work in a timely manner so life events won't get in the way. When you wait until the last minute to start your work, even a minor crisis can make you late.

The End Note:

Before I close, I want you to realize that late work doesn't only affect you. I've said before that your prof likely teaches more than one class, unless she's a true part-timer who has another full-time job. Either way, that's a lot of grading, and your professor will address your late work whenever she can fit it in. It wouldn't be fair to other students who submitted work on time to put your late assignment first, would it? Also, your prof's review may be less thorough than the review you'd receive for work turned in on time. Depending on the degree of lateness, she may simply put a grade on it with no explanation as to why you received that grade.

I'm not asking you to feel sorry for us—this is our job, after all. But you should know that late work is a shared issue: You and your prof are partners in this educational process. We all realize life takes its unexpected turns. If you find yourself needing to submit an assignment after the deadline, your best measure is to own up to it, propose your course of action, and try not to make lateness a habit.

(I probably don't need to remind you about that work ethic ... but I guess I just did).

Chapter 17

Conflict with Work in Other Classes

What You Might Say:

I can't come to class because I have a monster test to study for in biology.

What Your Professor Thinks:

The work in my class is apparently less important to you than your monster test in biology.

The Real Story

Indira sent me an e-mail saying, "I'm going to have to miss class tonight. I have a bunch of work to do in my other class, and I have to get it done."

That same week, Canessa approached me about an hour into our daytime class (we meet for over two hours), and asked, "Can I leave early?"

"This is college," I said, matter-of-factly, but not in a sharp or angry tone (because I wasn't angry—I just knew I couldn't honor her request without ticking off 26 other students.). "If you need to leave early, then you have to make that decision. But out of fairness to the other people here, I can't say, 'Sure! Go ahead and leave early. No problem!'"

Canessa looked worried. "I really don't want to leave class, but my work schedule changed and now I don't have as much time to work on a major paper I have due in a couple of days."

I reiterated my point: I couldn't give her permission to leave early, but if that was the choice she needed to make, it was her decision.

The Back Story

I often wonder how students can so casually and candidly admit they need extra study time for another class—instead of being in mine. I mean, do you really want your friend who won't go see "The Hangover, Part 2" with you to blatantly say, "No thanks, I'd rather go to that party with Gregg"?

Obviously, you conclude Gregg made a better offer. You also may tell yourself, "I'm not as important as Gregg."

Granted, I'm comparing a college situation to a personal one, and professors don't take personal offense when you say you aren't staying in their class. Sure, there's a moment of, *Oh, so that other classwork is more important to you than this one? You obviously feel this class is worth missing*, but that's a professional complaint, rather than a personal one. However, when you freely admit you're prioritizing another class, your professor *does* think you perceive her class as miss-able.

On one hand, I guess students believe that since they're doing schoolwork, rather than, say, going to the club, the absence might be considered more acceptable. One prof should support the student of another prof, right? Certainly, we know our class isn't the only one you're taking, but we expect you know that, too. I've heard many students complain, "Professors give us so much work. Don't they realize we have other classes ... and lives?"

Yes, we totally realize that, but we have requirements for *our* classes. Most profs strive to assign meaningful work that matters to the overall course goals (remember those objectives I talked about?).

Another complaint students have is, "Why is my prof giving me this 10-page paper at the same time I have a mid-term and a major project? Why can't they all give these big assignments at different times?"

Unfortunately, college doesn't work that way. Each prof follows the same academic calendar; mid-terms and finals fall at the same time for everyone. It's not like all the profs sit in a big room and conspire to make your life miserable by giving you huge papers and exams during the same week.

(What would that even look like, anyway? All of us in black cloaks, plotting our 10-page papers and 100-question exams, while drinking bubbling brew and saying, "Muhahahahahahah!!!"? Crazy!)

Each professor needs to cover specific content before you take a mid-term or tackle that big project. Similarly, your prof may assign a huge research paper as an end-point of what you learned in class. How could he assign the paper any earlier than the final weeks of school if the knowledge has to happen ahead of time? Again, this is an unrealistic expectation of college.

Your profs want you to think about each of your classes in the same way you perceive every one of your closest friends: Equally important. Just as you try to devote a fair and balanced amount of time to each of those friends, your profs expect you to fairly arrange the workload of the classes you chose to take.

A prof can't give you leeway on his work because of your obligations in other classes. That's not reasonable and threatens your education and experience in *that* prof's class.

I know you may be thinking, *That's not fair. I can't handle all this work with my horrible schedule!* College won't be the last time you experience conflicting deadlines. Later on, you may have multiple projects to manage at work, or a group of employees who all need you at once.

Right now is the time to accept the fact that each class demands time and attention. Consider this when you register for classes, speak with your academic adviser, and confer with professors who teach classes you want to take: Ask yourself if you can handle the combined workload.

If you aren't sure, grab a syllabus from each class you're considering and see if you're signing up for the right combination of courses, based on your other obligations. If possible, don't take a group of classes that will suck up all your resources. If you *do* choose to have such a schedule, then at least you'll know what you're getting yourself into.

And let's return to reality: The reason you're asking to leave class doesn't matter to your professor, so don't ask to leave class early, because your prof won't be able to give you permission, anyway.

I hate to say it, but if you find yourself in a crunch, it's almost better to take a day off from class altogether rather than ask your prof for a free pass. For instance, if you're doing well in your Environmental Science class, haven't missed any days, and believe you can make up for the day you miss, you may save more time and energy by staying out and working on something else. Only you can weigh the consequences of this decision. But the bottom line is, don't expect your prof to do it for you. If you give yourself a day off under the premise of working on other classwork, make sure you use the time for that, rather than a trip to the mall.

Ask Yourself This:

Do I have a habit of overcommitting myself and then scrambling to keep up? Am I being realistic about the time I need for my classes, based on other things I have going on in my life? Am I willing to adjust my work schedule, my family obligations, or my social schedule in order to give each class the time it needs? Do I have a habit of skipping class or leaving early to work on another class? What are the typical reasons this happens?

Think This:

Each of my classes will take time. The amount of time depends on the number of assignments and exams and how easy or challenging I find the material. I need to know if I can handle the type of classes I'm taking, or if I should mix things up by taking different classes? I need to do research to figure this out. I'll feel much calmer when I know what I'm getting myself into.

Not That:

If I fall behind, I can blow off my chemistry class. I'm doing okay there.

Sure, you can blow off chemistry, but what if that one day you miss puts you behind? Or,

My prof will understand. He went to school too, and he knows I have a ton of work.

Your prof does understand, and he probably made tough decisions himself about attending (or not attending) classes to finish extra work. Your prof may have paid dearly for those decisions he made, too.

Say This:

I'm going to miss class on Tuesday.

Or,

I missed class last Tuesday. I looked at the schedule and see you covered Chapter 12. I've already read that chapter and feel I'm in good shape.

Or, you can say,

I missed class, but I've reviewed the material and I have a couple of specific questions.

You don't need to tell your prof you missed to study for another class. Again, the reason doesn't matter.

If you do fall into a situation where you have major assignments at the same time, the *second* you know about the assignments, meet with each prof individually and say,

> I have a major test, big paper, and project due in three different classes. I'm really struggling with how to schedule my time on these and give them all the attention they deserve. Can you help me set smaller goals so this won't seem so impossible?

Your prof can absolutely tell you what to focus on first, second, and third—a checklist so you can see your progress as you go. You'll feel less overwhelmed if you can mark off the small steps and feel you're gaining traction, rather than focusing on the big picture for all three assignments.

Not That:

> I need to miss class because I have a big test to study for.

Your prof doesn't need this information. Or,

> I couldn't get your paper finished because I had a paper due in another class.

Your prof will know you didn't schedule your time well. Don't tie your paper into the fact that you had to complete work for another class.

The End Note

All your profs have been in your shoes and can be your allies in creating a strategy to complete your assignments. However, a prof can't manage the actual time you devote to those tasks, or whether you scan Facebook during the time you set aside for schoolwork.

Many of your fellow students are also in your shoes. While you may feel no one understands how you're struggling, you are absolutely not alone. Ask fellow students to share ideas about staying on track with assignments. At the least, if you talk about your scheduling challenges with classmates, you may be able to report your progress to each other and keep each other accountable ... even on Facebook.

Chapter 18

Leaving Early or Arriving Late

What You Might Say:

May I leave 30 minutes early today? I have an appointment.

What Your Professor Thinks:

I can't give you permission to leave early without ticking off 32 other students in this class.

The Real Story

I've mentioned before that my night class meets once a week for three and a half hours. Barrie came up to me on a break and said, "I have a terrible headache and feel like I'm going to throw up. Can I go home?"

Earlier that day, before class ever began, Dionne e-mailed saying she had to work an hour later than usual and would need to arrive late.

Simon came to that evening's class, caught me before we even started, and said, "My girlfriend needs a ride home from work and I have to leave early. Am I going to miss very much?"

Most students don't realize profs have already heard all 1,872+ reasons why students need to leave class early or come in late.

The Back Story

I would rather be challenged on a grade 10 times over again than be asked "Can I leave early today?" Certainly, I understand there are occasions when students legitimately need to cut class short (or come in late). I also appreciate students' courtesy in telling me they need to leave class before it ends. Unexpected situations occur all the time. I know many students must work while in school, and many supervisors will not compromise to accommodate their schedules.

Yet the fact remains that students choose class times. Your professors need to know you perceive your college education as a job, too. You may not lose money when you're late to class or miss a class, but you do lose in other ways: lost points, missed work, and a challenged relationship with your professor.

Just as I have to arrange my life to teach at particular times, I anticipate my students will arrange their lives to be in class at the times they've chosen. I expect them to be present for as many *entire* class sessions as possible.

Before I move on, let me share one other reason students ask to leave early or come in late: Scheduling two classes close together. That's right: I've taught at 5:15 p.m. and had students ask if they can arrive fifteen minutes late because their previous class ends at 5:30 p.m. This means they tried to strike a "leave early" deal with the other prof. There's no way a professor can justify allowing this, even though I agree it's unfortunate for the student who needs to take both classes.

So, remember, regardless of the reason for leaving early, know that your prof can never say, "Yes, absolutely, please leave whenever you need to," without giving that option (or potentially ticking off) the other students in the class.

I usually tell students, "This is college. You don't need my approval to leave early. It's your choice when you come and go, so do what you need to do."

Then the inevitable question from the student: "But will I lose points?"

Now this is where things get sticky. Many students view leaving early (or being late) for class and staying in class for the full time as one and the same.

Seriously!

I've had students sit in class for ten minutes and then leave, expecting to receive credit for attending the whole time. Similarly, some students walk into class 15 minutes before the end, as though to say, "Hey, I showed my face for a few minutes. At least I was here!"

Some professors take attendance at the beginning of class and never look at the end to see who is still there. Others take attendance at the end to avoid the leaving early question altogether. Some profs don't take attendance at all. You do need to know that attendance points may be bundled with participation points, and even if they aren't, many professors will remember if you left significantly early and may take that into consideration when calculating your overall grade.

Ask Yourself This:

Do I frequently leave classes early or ask to leave early? What is my typical reason? Did I need to leave early in those situations, or did I just not want to stay in class? What consequences have I faced from leaving early in the past? If I think about the reasons I left early, were they reasonable? Was there anything I could do to avoid them? What scheduling changes can I make in the future to remain in class for the entire time?

(These questions also apply to coming into class late).

Think This:

I can leave early once or twice in a quarter for a valid reason and it probably won't have much effect on my standing in the class. However, my professor cannot give me permission to leave. I will take responsibility for any penalties I face for leaving early. Most of all, I will take a hard look at my schedule and make sure I have enough time to be in class and fulfill my other obligations on time.

Not That:

The prof won't notice if I leave early.

That may be true, but chances are the prof *will* know. Even if he doesn't know your name, he'll see you walk out the door.

It's my class time and if I don't want to stay for the whole thing, that's my business. I'm paying for this.

Absolutely true. Class time is yours, and you *are* paying for it. Therefore, don't you want to get the most benefit for your money (or financial aid)? Even if the class totally sucks, you still need the information you receive during class in order to do your work and get your grade.

I have a good reason for leaving early.

As I've said before in these chapters, the "why" doesn't matter. Not because your professor doesn't care, but because there's a job to be done and you both signed on to do it.

Say This:

Ideally, as soon as you know you need to leave early, tell the professor,

> Professor Jones, a situation has come up and I need to leave class early today. I know this isn't ideal. I don't plan on making this a regular habit.

If you're further into the term, you can add,

> As you know, I don't make it a habit of leaving early. I understand I may face a penalty for this and I'm willing to be responsible for any work I missed.

Or,

> Professor, I'm going to be late on Thursday. It's unavoidable and I'll keep my overall lateness to a minimum. I've reviewed the schedule, and I see we're going to cover Chapter 5 that day. I'll be sure to start on Chapter 5 and catch myself up to where the class is when I arrive.

Not That:

> Can I leave early because _____?

Remember, your prof can't give you permission unless everyone else in the class has the option to leave with you. Or,

> I shouldn't lose attendance points because I came in late or left early. That's not fair!

Every individual professor has the right to impose reasonable class management policies. If your class involves group or paired work, your professor needs to have every student present for the full time so those activities will go smoothly. If your prof maintains a stiff attendance policy that includes late arrival/early departure, she has a good reason.

The End Note

The late/early issue frustrates professors. We may empathize with you, but we're also trying to maintain fairness for all students. What we're really talking about is the general debate over attendance policies in college. Some people think college should not include attendance-taking—that students who show up will naturally do better than those who don't, and the decision is individual. Other people think it's a necessary practice to keep students accountable and allow for community building in the classroom. Regardless, know the attendance policy for each of your classes (find it in the syllabus) and determine where leaving early and coming in late falls within that policy. If you're unsure, ask your professor to clarify the guidelines.

By handling your early/late situation proactively without asking for special treatment, you'll maintain a better working relationship with your professor. You may even receive more leniency. And if not, at least you approached the situation like a professional.

Chapter 19

Going Over What You Missed

What You Might Say:

I was out last Thursday. Can you tell me everything I missed?

What Your Professor Thinks:

Do you expect me to hold a private class and cover 50 minutes worth of material—again?

The Real Story

Michael sent me an e-mail saying, "I think I have the flu. Can you send me everything I'm going to miss from class today?"

I e-mailed back, "Michael, I'm sorry you're sick. I recommend you look at the class schedule and see what chapters we're working on. Everything you need is in the course management system, so you should be able to bring yourself up to speed. If you review the chapters or assignment and find you have specific questions after doing so, I'm glad to answer them for you."

Then this from Michael: "But can't you just send me what I need? I am really not feeling well and it would just be easier."

Michael obviously wasn't following my encouragement to take charge of the situation.

My response: "Michael, the schedule is under the Syllabus tab, you have your textbook, and you can find the assignment in the Course

Modules section. I know you don't feel well, but you can find this information pretty quickly once you're feeling better. You'll want to know your way around the course management system, so this will be good practice. Again, I'm glad to answer questions after you go through the chapter and assignment."

I didn't hear back from Michael, but I know he located what he needed because he turned in his assignment.

Eve missed a week of class, reason unknown. She came into my office during office hours and said, "Could you go over what I missed?"

I replied (and although this comment may *sound* sarcastic, I made every effort to not let my tone sound that way and I smiled when I said it), "Do you mean I should repeat class all over again?"

Eve laughed, "No, of course not, but do you think you can go over what the class did?"

I asked Eve if she had her syllabus/class schedule with her. She didn't. I pulled one up on my computer and printed it. Then, I repeated what I said to Michael:

"Here's the schedule and you'll be able to see what we covered on the days you were out. Please take a look at those chapters and the assignment and then come back to me with any questions that you have."

Fortunately, Eve wasn't resistant. "Oh, okay," she said casually, as if she never thought of doing this.

The Back Story

Would you ask your Rabbi, Priest, or Minister to repeat last week's sermon just for you in your living room because you missed the service?

I bet you wouldn't.

Your prof cannot and will not hold a mini make-up class for you in her office either. But this sounds like what you're asking your prof to do in order to "go over what you missed." I think students revert to their elementary or secondary years when a friend or parent could pick up a packet of work when you were gone. College just doesn't work this way. All-inclusive packets of material are rarely available to catch you up after an absence. If you miss class, it's always up to you to gather the information yourself. Your first step is to look at the planned class schedule and see what happened while you were away. Actually, I'm shocked by how few students refer to the class schedule before asking if I can give them a full recap of the day's events.

If the schedule says the class went over Chapter 6, then it isn't too difficult to figure out what you should do, right? Read Chapter 6! If your professor posts lecture notes, PowerPoint files, or other associated multimedia in a course management system, such as Moodle or BlackBoard, then you should be able to find the material you missed and take responsibility for catching yourself up.

Bottom line? Before you ever approach your professor with the question of what you missed, be proactive and view that information first. From there, you can ask a classmate or two who attended class if they'll share notes from the day's events. Notice I said the "day's" events. If you were gone more than a day or two, you need to schedule an appointment with your professor during office hours to determine your overall status in the class. If you can stay, you still have a responsibility to update yourself on any reading or assignments. You'll want to find out ahead of time if you can use any late penalty to your advantage (meaning, to help you remain in the class, rather than having to drop or fail it).

Let's get back to missing one day here or there: After you review any classwork that's available, then, and only then, should you contact your professor to ask further questions. You can either e-mail or visit during office hours, preferably before your next scheduled class. Translation: Do not pop into the prof's office right before class is about to begin or launch into an elaborate discussion in the classroom just minutes before class.

Ask Yourself This:

What do I usually do about missed work? Do I take responsibility to catch myself up? Do I expect the teacher to do it for me? How has this worked in other situations? In the past, have I fallen behind because I did not take responsibility to track down missed work? How did falling behind make me feel? What consequences did I suffer? Have there been times when I took full responsibility to get myself on track? Did I feel confident, proud of myself, and responsible?

Think This:

Whether the absence was avoidable or unavoidable, any time I miss something in class, it's always my responsibility to find out what I missed. I can ask a classmate and look at course-related documents to figure out what I need to work on. If I have questions after doing those things, then I can ask my professor for help.

Not That:

It's the professor's job to catch me up. It's not my fault I missed class.

A professor's job is to *teach* class, not *re*-teach class. Even with your valid absence, the professor's requirement to teach class one time, to the best of his/her ability, doesn't change. Or,

The professor will probably go over everything again, so I can just catch up at the next class.

This may be true, but you may also find that the class moved on. If you raise your hand in class and say, "I missed class, so could you go over that again?" your classmates will probably roll their eyes and groan. They already sat through the lesson once.

Say This:

Professor, I missed your class on Wednesday. I looked at the schedule and noticed you covered Chapter 6 that day. I reviewed the material myself and asked Joann, who sits next to me, for the notes. I'm a bit confused on (insert specific question here) and would like to ask some questions.

Or,

Professor, I missed your class on Wednesday. I looked at the schedule and noticed you covered Chapter 6 that day. I read Chapter 6 and also received information about the assignment from Joann, who sits next to me. I think I'm in good shape with catching up, but just want to make sure I haven't missed anything else.

Not That:

Can you tell me what I missed?

Or,

Can you go over what I missed?

Or,

What should I do now?

Remember, the prof cannot and will not hold class again for you. What you should do is take action yourself before you ask further questions. The materials should be at your disposal, either via your schedule, another classmate, or other online course support. If you can't find something, then you can ask for further help locating what the class went over.

The End Note

Sometimes the ideal happens with students and absences. Rahim had a sudden, unexpected opportunity to take a trip overseas with his family. He met with me and said, "Mrs. Bremen, I'm going to miss two classes, but I looked at the schedule and already printed out the assignments from the chapters you're covering. I have a few days before I leave, so I'll read this weekend. I don't believe I'll fall behind. I think I can even have a draft of my outline to you before I go."

Wow. Rahim assigned his own early deadlines to make up for his time out of the classroom; he was not expecting me to take action for his decision.

Another example, and while this is going to seem unreal, it is absolutely true (and not while I was teaching in Vegas either!): A young mother told me that she was going to miss class the following week because she had "a pole dancing competition where she was a finalist and stood to win $10,000." (Yes, the competition was in Vegas). She was completely business-like about the situation, had all her work done in advance, and other than missing the day of class (the day of the actual competition), she never missed one assignment. I don't think she won the competition, unfortunately.

As I've said before, and I'll say again: Your professor will be much kinder and far more responsive if, instead of asking her to be REactive and feed you everything you missed, you show her you are PROactive and responsible.

Chapter 20

Figuring Out if You Missed
Something "Important"

What You Might Say:

I was out last Thursday. Did I miss anything important?

What Your Professor Thinks:

I work very hard to prep for class. I don't present material that's unimportant.

The Real Story

Clare missed a few days of class due to being out of town. She dutifully showed up in my office after her absences and said, "Did I miss anything important while I was gone?"

I won't say how I responded because I'm always at a loss for words when this question arises—and I'm rarely at a loss for words.

Owen checked in with me on the phone during the afternoon before my evening class. "I have a family emergency," he said. "I looked at the schedule and it doesn't seem we're covering anything big tonight, so I won't be missing much, will I?"

Now I know my class schedule is detailed, particularly since this night class meets for fewer class sessions, but for a longer period of time. I often tell my students that skipping one class is like missing the equivalent of four. In my mind, I questioned how Owen came to the conclusion that in our four hours' worth of class, we wouldn't be doing anything worthwhile.

The Back Story

Long ago, when I shared an office, a colleague of mine and I tossed around what we *wished* we could say to students in response to "Did I miss anything important?"

I won't share what we came up with because it isn't appropriate for these pages. I will admit it was delicious to fantasize.

"Did I miss anything important today?" is probably the #1 most offensive question for professors. I believe students have no idea how the statement comes across. When students ask if they've missed anything important, they believe it's a *good* thing to wonder about that. Students want validation that missing class was *okay* (translation: justified) because nothing particularly important to their success happened (or will happen) that day. For example, we didn't review for a major test. Ninety-nine percent of students would consider *that* important information, not to be missed.

Although students often feel like they're putting in seat time—a fixed number of hours where important information is only conveyed on certain days, the truth is that most professors work hard to plan a meaningful class session for you. Even if your prof has been teaching for 50 years and recycles material term after term, she still has to glance over what she'll be discussing and may need to make copies. Granted, that isn't a ton of prep, but it is prep nonetheless.

Other professors recognize they need to work harder every year to earn students' attention. So, they create elaborate PowerPoint presentations, locate YouTube videos or other multimedia, or pore over publisher's instructor manuals to find the right classroom activity to drive home their points. And this is for one or two days' worth of lessons.

Imagine if your prof is trying to plan new instruction for every single class session. We're talking an incredible number of work hours—often on the prof's own time. Colleges don't give profs dedicated prep time like high school teachers, and we juggle it in tandem with committee meetings, service to our college, community, research, meeting with students, and other duties. To your professor, whatever prep she goes through to make your classroom time meaningful is *extremely* important.

Let's look at this another way: Maybe your prof isn't planning a big instructional day, but he's returning papers he spent all his weeknights grading. He wants to go over the results with the entire class and talk about problem areas. Now, your course schedule doesn't say this because your prof may have just made the plan. Your prof is going to perceive this return-your-grade day as critical. And it should be to you, as well. But, remember, you probably looked at the schedule and didn't know something this important was coming.

Believe it or not, even if you're missing a low-key day where the class is doing little work, it's still good for you to be there. In fact, days like that are as important as others because you're building community, having impromptu discussion about classwork, or participating in activities that will help you engage with your content in a different way—and maybe even understand it more clearly.

Even if absolutely nothing you consider to be important happens on a particular day, the fact is this: You're in college. You paid (or someone is paying) for you to be in class. In high school, you may have had slack days where you played games or everyone read to themselves silently. Maybe your teacher planned those "dead days," or maybe the teacher just needed to pass required time for you to be there.

In college, your professor is expected to give you dedicated instruction. Not every class session will be riveting. Not every session will feel important to you. Hell, some days you may feel so bored you want to pull out your arm hairs one by one just to stay awake. Regardless, the time is important.

Ask Yourself This:

When I think back to high school classes, what days did I feel were not important? Have I accepted that college classes typically contain information that's helpful for my learning, even if I don't see it that way at the time? How do I decide what information is important? If I've done this in college, have I been correct? Or did I end up missing something I shouldn't have missed?

Think This:

I have a class schedule available to me, but the professor could make changes to it. If I try to figure out whether an upcoming class will cover something I need, I may miss something that was unscheduled. I should make every effort to attend as many classes as possible and, even if I'm bored, I'll try to find something valuable about that particular class.

(Even if the only valuable aspect was that you actually showed up—because that is important.)

Not That:

It won't make much of a difference if I miss this day. We probably aren't doing anything important.

Like I said, you just never know.

Say This:

If you absolutely must gauge whether or not one day is more "important" than another to miss, say,

> Professor, I have to miss next Thursday and I apologize for that. I've tried to keep my absences to a minimum (only say this if it's true). I looked at the schedule and I see you're covering Chapter 11 that night. I know we're taking our quiz a few days later. I believe I'll be able to stay on track. Is there anything I'm not thinking about that may be covered that night? I'd be glad to do the research on my own or ask a classmate to help me with notes.

Not That:

Did I miss anything important?

After reading my discussion of this topic, you'll remove this sentence from your phrase vault, right? I hope so!

The End Note

Remember what I said about your work ethic in college being a sign of your overall work ethic? (How could you forget?) If that's the case—and I firmly believe it is—then because you were in class, because you showed up, the class day was important.

And if you weren't there? Regard that day as important to your professor and the other people in your class. Why?

Because they were there, so it was important to them.

Chapter 21

Apologizing

What You Might Say:
> I'm sorry I didn't turn my paper in on time.

What Your Professor Thinks:
> Don't tell me you're sorry. It isn't my education that's on the line.

The Real Story

Apologies from students come in many different forms: Verona says, "I'm so sorry I didn't turn in my assignment on time."

"I didn't expect to fail that test," Jonah explains. "I'll try to do better."

Sometimes students' apologies reflect the feeling that we, their professors, are disappointed in them. I'll explain: One strong student, Derek, who had taken several classes with me, did a weak presentation in front of a group of high school students. I later learned he didn't practice as much as he wanted and didn't adjust his content the way we discussed.

When I evaluated Derek, I noted the issues and said, "I've seen you do many speeches, but this one seemed like a struggle in terms of the organizational flow. Also, you didn't seem comfortable with your delivery."

Derek was scheduled for another high school speech the following week. That one went much better, presented with his typical dynamism and flair, plus solid content. He received his usual "A". Later, when applying for a scholarship Derek wrote a personal essay about a prof he'd learned the most from. He asked me to review the document for him. To my surprise, he wrote about me—the time he did a poor presentation and felt he'd disappointed me. I contacted Derek immediately and said, "My feedback to you wasn't personal. I wasn't disappointed in you; I was disappointed in the product. My feedback was not personal. It was based on the requirements for that speech."

"I really thought I disappointed you," Derek said. "I wanted to do better, and I felt like I really let you down."

The Back Story

Saying "I'm sorry" is definitely a courtesy in our society, so when a student perceives she's done something wrong, I'm not surprised when the first instinct is to apologize. I'm never sure how to respond when a student says she's sorry.

I can't say, "Oh, that's okay," even though that's my first instinct. To be honest, what the student is apologizing for is often *not* okay. I don't mean okay with me … I mean okay in general. Is it okay for a student to do poorly on a test? The student's grade isn't going to be okay, and her comprehension was clearly not okay.

See where I'm going with this? I've been tempted to say, "Don't apologize to me. This isn't *my* education we're talking about. I've already graduated. This is *your* education!"

Does that sound harsh? I'm trying to convey that a student never, ever, ever has to satisfy or please me. I realize the student-professor dynamic seems similar to a parent-child relationship. But I've said it before: Students and their profs are partners in the educational process.

Yes, I know the professor is the one doing the grading—and seemingly the judging, but our judgments are not personal (although it may feel that way). They're an evaluation of how well you're mastering the objectives and standards of the course.

Sometimes, students will run speech topic ideas by me, asking, "Which one do you like best?"

My immediate response is, "What topic do *you* like best? What topic do you feel passionate about? Which do you think will fit the assignment? Which topic can you find credible research on?"

I realize students are trying to seek my approval, but you don't need to do that. Instead, seek guidance, mentoring, and partnership. And with that, unless you say or do something unkind to your professor, you never, ever have to apologize.

Ask Yourself This:

Why do I feel I need to apologize to my professor? Do I think I've done something wrong? Has apologizing for not getting work done helped me in the past? Am I hoping the professor will be more lenient? Am I trying to be courteous?

Think This:

I've already caused myself extra stress by my performance. I don't need to apologize for anything. I need to do things differently next time. I will make a plan so I can.

Not That:

I do not need to apologize. This is what I learned to do when I've done something wrong.

Schoolwork is business. Saying how sorry you are implies your professor is personally disappointed in you, or you've done something wrong to him. You haven't. No need to say you're sorry.

Say This:

After you've clarified what needed to be done differently, say,

I didn't do my best on the last exam. I realize I'm confused about certain concepts and I needed to ask for help earlier. I'd like to meet with you to go over what I'm missing. I don't want to let this happen again.

Or,

I didn't finish my assignment. I waited too long to start it and then realized it took longer than I gave myself time for. I reviewed the late policy in the syllabus and plan to turn in the paper next week for a 50 percent penalty. I wanted to let you know and confirm I'm reading the policy correctly.

See? No apologies—only what you plan to do to remedy the situation. Nice and proactive!

Not That:

I'm sorry I didn't perform better.

No apologies needed. What are you going to *do* about it?

Or,

> I hope you're not disappointed in me.

Your prof is not your parent. He may have hopes for you to succeed, but he doesn't have personal investment like a family member.

The End Note:

Not that I asked him to, but Derek ended up rewriting part of his scholarship essay. He won the scholarship. We remain in contact to this day.

I can't say this enough: Profs are concerned about your success and well-being, but your performance in class does not change our lives. If an entire class is failing or flocks of students complain, yes, that could have a professional impact on us because our administration would wonder what's going on with our performance. Generally speaking, your prof has nothing personal to lose or gain based on your grades.

I've said it before: You are the owner of your education, not your professors. We've already finished our degrees—many of them.

This is *your* journey.

Communicate your needs to your professor. Even if your goals don't go as planned, always communicate intentions, rather than remorse.

Chapter 22

Frequent E-mailing

What You Might Do:

E-mail your prof 15 times in an hour when you haven't heard back from her.

What Your Professor Thinks:

E-mailing me every minute will not make me respond faster.

The Real Story

Tuesday, 9 a.m.

Ellen, I e-mailed you an hour ago and haven't heard back. I'm really stuck on my assignment and need your help. Please write back.

Marlee

Tuesday 10:30 a.m.

Ellen, I still haven't heard back from you and I really can't figure this out. I know the draft of our research paper is due later today. I need to hear from you!

Marlee

Tuesday, 12:25 p.m.

Ellen, I don't understand what's going on. Aren't you supposed to be a little more available on a day when a major paper is due? Guess I'm not going to do as well because I didn't hear from you.

Marlee

My response:

Tuesday, 12:43 p.m.

Marlee, I apologize for not getting in touch with you sooner. I had an early meeting that ran from 9-10 a.m. and then I got a call that my daughter was sick and needed to be picked up from school. I have just now gotten back to e-mail.

While I empathize that you're having confusion over the paper and need help, let me point out two things:

First, my e-mail response policy says 24-hours, so although I usually respond quickly, I do have that time window available.

Second, if you needed help on the paper, we're both at a disadvantage to discuss that on the day it's due. How will you have time to implement major changes and how can I give your paper the time it deserves?

Since the paper is due today, we're outside of the window where I can review it more thoroughly. If you have a specific question, I can try to answer it for you.

Thank you,

Ellen

Here's another typical exchange:

Friday, 10:47 p.m.

Ellen,

I know our quiz is due tonight at midnight and my Internet isn't working! I don't know what's going on. It was working fine all day and just now locked up. Just want to let you know I've trying to get this quiz done.

Thanks,

Steven

Friday, 11:28 p.m.

Ellen,

Still can't get online and really don't know what to do. You won't get this e-mail till the morning and by then it will be too late to submit. If you possibly get this, can you tell me what my options are?

Thanks,

Steven

Saturday, 12:35 a.m.

Ellen,

Finally got back online and just submitted my quiz. I hope you'll still accept it.

G'night,
Steven

Saturday, 8:00 a.m.

Ellen,

Just wanted to make sure you got my other e-mails. I have to go to work, but I hope you can get back to me and let me know if you got the quiz. My Internet was still giving me trouble, but I think it was sent.

Thanks,
Steven

Saturday 9:05 a.m.

Hi, Steven,

I'm sorry to hear about the trouble you were having with your Internet. I was sleeping at the time you were e-mailing, so it was impossible for me to respond sooner. I'm glad you were able to get the quiz submitted, but I hope you may reconsider when you're getting these done in the future. I know whenever I wait until the last minute, it's almost a sure sign I'm risking something going wrong. How about building in some time for these types of emergencies?

Regarding the quiz, check it again. If you get a message that says "already submitted," you are likely good to go. I can check the actual score by Monday.

Have a good weekend,
Ellen

The Back Story

Some colleagues tell me they've had students e-mail every 15 minutes and become angrier and angrier when they don't get a response. As you can imagine, e-mail has impacted communication between students and professors in a big way. Professors are expected to give on-demand service, 24-hours a day, seven days a week via e-mail.

And you know what?

Some professors *are* on e-mail early mornings, weekends, and late evenings, even during holidays. A lot of us accept our jobs changing along with technology. I teach partly online now and partly in the classroom. Of course, my online students expect ready service since we're using this delivery model to accommodate other life challenges we both face. What's interesting is that when I taught daily in the classroom, students anticipated the same speedy e-mail response.

Most profs give themselves a 12 to 24-hour response window, with the exception of weekends or holidays. Sure, a prof may respond in a moment, an hour, or two hours, but consider that a bonus. Many students think their profs teach class, hang out in our offices, then go home. Any prof will tell you that the time spent teaching is really the shortest part of our job. Let me give you a sample of a professor's responsibilities:

1. Teach classes. Maybe one or several, which could be any hour of the day or night.
2. Build curriculum—on our own time.
3. Work with departments/divisions. Schedule planning, program-build, discuss curriculum. May involve monthly, bi-monthly, and/or weekly meetings.
4. Serve as student advisers.
5. Serve on campus committees. Meetings can vary from weekly to monthly.
6. Maintain professional involvement in organizations and advisory boards. This may include attending meetings, submitting conference papers and presentations (which take time to develop or research), serving on the board, etc.
7. Contribute to and attend campus events. Organize teaching events on campus, such as brown bag discussions, workshops, etc., attend symposiums, intellectual or social gatherings, host clubs.
8. Community involvement. Contractual obligation at some colleges: Forging and maintaining connections with area high schools, community organizations, etc.
9. Service to the community. Also contractual at some colleges.

I've only listed nine items here, but each can require layers of outside work, numerous people to network with, and hours of report writing. Also, notice I didn't even mention a prof's e-mail management. At times I go off to an hour-long meeting and return to find 23 e-mails from students and colleagues. Each one takes time to answer.

So, when you e-mail your prof and wonder why you haven't received a response in a minute, do not automatically assume you are being ignored. Think about it: Why would your prof *want* to let your e-mail sit in his/her in-box? She'll only have to deal with it later. Unfortunately, there are no firm standards for a professor to reply to your e-mails. Most colleges do not write a policy on this in a prof's contract, as far as I know.

How will you know your professor's e-mail response policy? Simple! Look in the syllabus. If you don't see any information that relates to e-mail communication, then ask (I'll tell you how, of course!). Once you see that your prof commits to e-mailing you back within two hours, 10 hours, or 24-hours—whatever the case may be—don't become impatient when he doesn't answer you before then.

If that time passes, you have a right to follow up and ask if your original e-mail was received. But, it's courteous to give your prof a window of time, maybe even double what he sets as the guideline, except if the guideline is 24 hours. In other words, if the prof says she'll respond in two hours, give her four and then check in to see if she got your e-mail.

I want to be clear on something before I move on to the next tip: If your professor has a specified turnaround time for e-mail response, it's up to you to adjust *your* schedule to it—not the other way around. Let's say you have a paper due and you want your prof to review it. Your prof won't guarantee checking e-mail on weekends more than once. If the only time you have to work on your paper is the weekend, then it's up to *you* to adjust your timeline. Work on that paper early so you can receive feedback in a timeframe your professor has already set, rather than staying hung up all weekend because you missed your prof's one-e-mail-check-per-weekend rule.

Okay, now on to the next recommendation: Only e-mail your prof after you've already used at least *two* other means to answer the question yourself.

Quite often (as in, about 75 percent of the time), the information a student is looking for can be found in a syllabus or within a course management system or course website. Profs become frustrated when you don't take the time to dig a little and locate information for yourself. In fact, when a student asks me about a policy that's clearly outlined in the syllabus, I usually say, "Go check your syllabus and after you do, I'll be glad to answer questions for you."

I'm not trying to be bitchy by doing this. I always tell students I want them to get familiar with all the materials for our class because I know what good practice this is. Students increase their confidence when they can locate answers for themselves. Likewise, if you're seen as a student who usually tries to find your own answers, when you have real questions you'll be taken much more seriously.

Know that you can also ask another student for help. If you genuinely can't figure something out and neither can your colleague, then your prof needs to know about your confusion. Think about it: When you're working, you won't go to your boss with every little question. You'll want to show that you can tackle issues yourself, so you'll only approach the supervisor for things that are out of your league. So, if you are struggling to find good research for a paper, go to a librarian and ask for help. If you aren't sure your paper sounds clear, have a close friend or family member take a look *before* asking your prof. Then, make that paper the best it can be before you ask your prof for a review. You want to catch any simple issues yourself so your prof can focus on what could *really* tank your grade.

Two last notes before I close this section: Another reason students rapid-fire e-mail professors: Because they want their grade! Right! Now!!!! You do have a right to receive graded work in a reasonable period of time, but you are not within your rights to bug your professor via e-mail and keep nagging unless an unreasonable amount of time has passed.

Okay, last tip: Before you accuse your prof of not responding to an e-mail, make sure you're checking the correct e-mail. My college implemented a student e-mail system because too many students were not receiving correspondence through their personal e-mails, or they would change their e-mail address and not inform the college. When this procedure went into effect, a student e-mailed me from our course management system, but my response went directly to that student's *college* e-mail. The student checked his personal e-mail, didn't see a message from me, and then thought I hadn't responded.

Quick note here: If your course management system e-mail goes to an e-mail you don't check, ask the college help desk, IT department, or your prof if they can help you set a forward. Then, your e-mails will reliably go to a place you do check.

Ask Yourself This:

Why am I e-mailing my professor? Have I tried to find the information myself first? If I'm e-mailing my professor again, how much time have I allowed for a response? Did I look at the syllabus to read the e-mail response policy? Has that much time now passed? Did I leave myself enough time to have my question answered, or did I wait until the last minute and that's why I am asking my professor to e-mail me back so quickly?

Think This:

If the e-mail policy on the syllabus says the prof will respond the same day, then I have to give her a chance to do that. If I procrastinated, it is not my professor's responsibility to rescue me. I will have to wait to hear what the prof has to say and then deal with the time that I have left.

Not That:

It's my prof's job to answer my e-mail quickly!

Your professor's job is to respond to your e-mail within the time she sets.

It's not my fault something went wrong with my computer/Internet/paper/printer. The professor should be a little more available when there's a due date so he can help with last minute problems.

Your professor is required to be accessible to you a certain amount of time during a class week. Technically, no hard and fast requirement exists for e-mail availability, even when an assignment is due. I can't stress enough that you should always leave yourself enough time for unexpected crises.

Say This:

If you don't see an e-mail response policy on the syllabus, say,

Professor, I didn't notice anything on the syllabus stating how you respond to e-mails. Can you explain when we should expect to hear back from you if we e-mail you? Will you answer e-mails over the weekend? What about when assignments are due? How early should we e-mail you with questions or to ask for review?

If you need a response from your professor earlier than his stated response time, say,

Professor, I know you usually respond to e-mails in two to three hours and I appreciate that you often respond sooner. I have to work today and I have a specific question regarding our paper that's due next week. I'm trying to work on this early and I'm finding myself stuck with one part of the argument. I'd like to keep working on this early so I can get it to you for review within your 72-hour window.

If you've e-mailed the prof and haven't heard back within her stated response time, resend the e-mail and add,

Professor, I e-mailed you yesterday at 2 p.m. I know the syllabus states you'll respond within 24-hours and it's been a little longer than that. I'm wondering if you received my e-mail. I'd like to take care of the question I asked so I can move forward with this assignment.

Not That:

I need you to answer this e-mail now!

No, your professor doesn't have to e-mail you back now, no matter how much you need her to.

I can't believe you're not e-mailing me back!

Believe it! There is probably a good reason—maybe because it's the middle of the night? And you did check the correct e-mail address—right?

If I don't do well on this assignment, it will be because you didn't get back to me.

No ... it will happen because you didn't ask the question early enough for both of us to give your issue the time it probably needed.

Are you ignoring me?

Your prof isn't ignoring you, even though you may feel that way. Think about it logically: Why would your professor do that? He's going to have to deal with whatever issue you have sooner or later.

I really need to know what my grade is.

And you will, when your prof is finished grading. Responding to you is going to take time and delay her grading even further.

The End Note

I find it odd that I'm talking so much about e-mail when students are using it less and less in their lives. Texting and Facebook get far more attention, but until some widespread change happens, e-mail will likely remain the dominant form of communication between students and profs. Texting wouldn't make sense for class correspondence, and I personally don't believe Facebook is appropriate for class-related issues, such as grading (though this is an individual opinion and other profs may feel differently).

E-mail maintains a professional and "official" record of exchanges between students and professors, which is why it's important to think of e-mail as great practice for your future work life. So, don't abuse e-mail, but use it to expand productive and positive communication with your prof.

Believe me, your good e-mail habits will be recognized and greatly appreciated!

Chapter 23

Your E-mail Address

What You Might Do:
Have the e-mail address "Bootylicious775@xmail.com."

What Your Professor Thinks:
"Bootylicious775@xmail.com" is not a professional e-mail address. And I don't know who you are.

The Real Story
toyotajune@xmail.com
catbite@xmail.com
purpleclouds@xmail.com
blackviper227@xmail.com
Godschild@xmail.com
and…
vaginamacdonald@xmail.com

(Note: All e-mail addresses have been modified to protect the real students they represent, but I kept the general themes).

The Back Story
Who *are* these people? Your guess is as good as mine! What does a prof do when she receives an e-mail from catbite@xmail.com with no signature? I'll tell you what she does: Nothing!

If I can't identify who an e-mail comes from, then I have no idea where my response goes. Remember what I said in Chapter 1 about FERPA (that privacy act protecting your educational records)? I need to know an actual student is sending me a message and not, well, a purple cloud or black viper (because I don't think vipers send e-mails).

College is the place to start building your professional self. Many career experts call this branding. Should I even ask what your brand is saying about you when your e-mail is "bootielicious" or "vaginamacdonald"? Do I want to know? Many colleges will now assign you an e-mail based on your name. So, for example, mine would be ellenbremen@college.edu. Other colleges allow students to change the address to something more creative, but when the prof receives the e-mail, she only sees the student's actual name, not the actual e-mail address.

This is at least one step in the right direction, but if the prof needs to copy the e-mail address for some reason, there's "Godschild" or "thefourfortyfours" (or worse "vaginamacdonald") staring you right in the face.

Some colleges do not have student e-mail and the student uses any old e-mail address. This is where things get interesting because the prof could see something either totally inappropriate or completely incomprehensible. (True story: a student once had an e-mail address with all symbols and another student used all exclamation points). Without a signature, the prof has no clue who is sending the e-mail. Worse than that, the prof may get more information about a student than he ever wanted to know.

Taking this topic in a completely practical direction, colleges do filter e-mails. This means that "toyotajune" could end up in the school's junk mailbox or spam filter as being "promotional."

My recommendation is simple: Get a professional e-mail address that you only use for college business. You can use any variation of your name:

-ebremen

-ellen.bremen

-bremene

See how easy and personalized that is? If other people share your name, then attach a number to the e-mail address (ebremen1), or a middle name or initial (ellenbbremen). I know it doesn't feel jazzy, but that's okay. You'll be showing your professional self, which is what you want.

Ask Yourself This:

Getting really honest with myself, could my e-mail address give others a negative or questionable impression of me? What image do I *want* to present to others in a professional situation when they see my e-mail address?

Think This:

For e-mails with my friends or family, a funky e-mail address is fine. But college is business, and I should get an e-mail address that's professional. I want to keep all of my personal and college/work-related information separate anyway.

Not That:

Crap. If I have to create a professional e-mail address, that's just another place I have to check, and I really don't like e-mail anyway.

Guess what? Multiple e-mail accounts are going to be a part of your life for quite a while. Once you start working, you'll have yet another account to check. Get in the habit now.

Or,

It doesn't matter what my e-mail is. No one pays attention. I'll change it later.

You're right that an unknown e-mail address with no signature doesn't grab attention, but you won't get your questions answered either.

Say This:

To your college help desk/IT department:

Does the college give students e-mail addresses? Do I need to sign up for this or is it automatically assigned to me? Where does the e-mail from my course management system go? Will all official college correspondence go to this e-mail address?

To your professor if you sent an e-mail from an unknown e-mail address,

I e-mailed you on Wednesday and accidentally left my name off. You may not have been able to figure out who I am from my e-mail address. I just changed my address to my name. Would you like me to resend the message?

Not That:

I e-mailed you, but you didn't get back to me. Didn't you get it?

Your prof receives tons of e-mails each day. As I've said before, it isn't in your prof's best interest to ignore your e-mail. Check your sent file to see if you signed your e-mail and if your address was something your prof could connect to your identity. If not, that's why you didn't get a response.

The End Note

A few final thoughts here: First, your prof will probably *not* say, "Hey, get a professional e-mail address," but believe me, if you use something strange it will be noticed—for all the wrong reasons.

If your college doesn't provide you an e-mail address, and you use your own, but then change it, make sure you update your college record and also change the e-mail in your course management system. If you don't, you'll have a sparkly new e-mail address, but you'll miss important information.

Finally, I'll remind you again that nearly every e-mail service and your course management system allow e-mail forwarding so you don't have to check multiple accounts. Get that going immediately to save yourself time.

Okay! Now go set up your new e-mail address. Then you can tell everyone how professional you've become.

Chapter 24

Angry E-mails

What You Might Do:

Fire off a nasty-gram after receiving a grade you dislike, or over another issue.

What Your Professor Thinks:

I have a permanent record of these words. Have you considered the consequences of that?

The Real Story

E-mail #1:

Dear Ellen,

I didn't receive any response from you from my last e-mail, so I just sent another email about if I can pass or not. I really am a good student, it's just been a difficult quarter for me. I'm ready to do whatever it takes to pass, so please just let me know what exactly I need to do.

Thanks,

Christiana

Response #1:

Dear Christiana,

I'm sorry to hear that this has been a challenging term for you. I'm sure you are not alone—many other students and even a lot of your professors have gone through the same thing.

Because we're in week eight and your two major speeches required to pass the class are not complete, I need to know a timeline when you propose to get these done. They cannot be submitted together; you need to be able to build on the first one for the second one. Also, they will be subject to a late penalty.

Have you calculated your points so far to see if you can still pass once you turn these in with the late penalty? If you need help analyzing these calculations once you've looked at them, let me know.

Thanks,

Ellen

E-mail #2:

Ellen,

Wait, I don't understand. Why do I have to have a late penalty since it wasn't my fault I didn't get these done? Then I won't pass for sure. With only two weeks left in the term, I barely have enough time to finish these speeches and get my other class assignments done. Why can't I turn them in together? Can't you give me an extension?

Christiana

Response #2:

Dear Christiana,

I realize you're probably feeling very stressed about catching yourself up. Depending on how your other work goes, even with low grades on these speeches, you may still be able to pass the class. It would be unfair to the rest of your class for me to accept the speeches late without imposing a late penalty. I also can't give you an extension because there are only two weeks left in the term.

Why don't we meet and look over your grades together and figure out a plan?

Ellen

E-mail #3:

Ellen,

This is really bullshit. It's not my fault that some things *out of my control* happened to me. I think the rest of the class would understand. I don't know what you expect me to do. This really sucks that you're making me hurry and get these things done when I'm already having a rough time.

Like I said, I'm usually a very good student. Can't you give me a break?

Christiana

Response #3:

Dear Christiana,

First of all, I totally get that you're frustrated. However, at this point, we should not continue e-mail dialogue because it seems to be escalating. If the tone and content of your e-mail continues, I'm going to have to bring my division chair in on our conversation. Let's avoid that and work to solve the problem instead. When would you like to come to my office?

Ellen

The Back Story

Would it surprise you to know that this was a *mild* e-mail exchange? Yes, there's a curse word and some anger, but believe me, it isn't as bad as e-mails filled with hate and blame from the first word. It happens to professors all the time, I promise you.

I'll start with the practical discussion: Your college has a student handbook with a student code of conduct. Based on that code, I'm sure expressing anger, either in person or online, can have serious consequences for you. Sending a flaming email isn't worth the risk, because you'll face larger consequences to your overall college experience than the worst case scenario of your original problem. This is another time I'm going to ask you to be selfish: Is the short-term satisfaction of blasting your prof worth leaving a scar on your record?

Now let's discuss the other aspect of your angry e-mail: You're pissed! I won't suggest you ignore your feelings or act as if they don't matter, because they do.

Without getting too Oprah or Dr. Phil here, you need to figure out who you're really mad at. Is it all about your professor, or are you mostly angry at the situation and yourself? It's hard to write a nasty e-mail starting with "Dear Me," isn't it? If you're mad at yourself for not getting a better grade, not understanding what you're learning, missing too many days … or whatever … then mouthing off to your professor via e-mail isn't the answer. You *can* express sadness, disappointment, worry, and fear. Your prof will relate to those feelings more generously than if you try to blame *her* for what went wrong. If you're in turmoil about the situation, you can certainly say that, too: "I realize it isn't your fault, but I'm furious about the issue."

Finally, if you *are* mad at your prof, you can explain yourself professionally, specifically, and tactfully. Again, this approach will get you so much farther than dropping a cluster of F-bombs. Bad language will earn you a trip to a division chair's office, or possibly a meeting with a college dean. There, your behavior will be the first line of discussion—not your original problem.

Remember: You can absolutely assert yourself in a direct manner without tearing another person down.

Being assertive is an art worth cultivating and enhancing in college. After all, in the workplace, mouthing off to a supervisor can get you fired. So, start channeling your frustration into productive communication right now.

Let me give you one more tip here: Decide if your problem really *would* be better handled in person. Many heated e-mail exchanges and texts would never escalate the same way face-to-face. We feel a sense of security when firing off words on a keyboard (or keypad), and that security is less comforting when we have to look someone right in the eye. Whether you're upset about a grade, a personal problem affecting your work, your class structure or something you feel your prof did, this is not a discussion for e-mail. Instead, write down what you want to say, or make a list, and then bring it with you to the professor's office. Don't feel you can look at your prof's face in the four walls of his office? Fine. Call him on the phone during office hours. Voice-to-voice contact still lets you keep your anger in check—much more so than e-mail.

My last suggestion is important: Don't let anger cloud your judgment and stop you from following the appropriate chain of command. Let me explain. I had a student, Kellan, who was furious over a C grade on an outline. In an e-mail he sent to my division chair, the college vice president, the president, *and* the director of human resources, he claimed that I was biased against the topic, which was the reason for the poor grade. The HR director e-mailed the student and said resolving the matter had to start with the division chair. The president and vice president both forwarded their e-mails to the division chair asking her if she'd intervened yet. She hadn't, other than to contact me and hear my side of the story.

I told her the student's grade wasn't based on the topic, but on lack of structure. Point one covered something completely different than point two. Either point, developed more fully, could have made a killer focused speech. I had documentation to back me up: The written evaluation, where I explained the same thing to the student. The division chair went back to the student and asked if Kellan would like her to be present during a meeting with me.

For 95 percent of problems, that's where all student-prof disputes have to start: Between the student and the professor. From there, a division chair can get involved, and if the issue is still not taken care of, a dean or VP may come into the picture.

Kellan clearly wanted me to get in major trouble, which was the reason for e-mailing everyone other than the President of the United States.

Did I get in trouble? No. The fault didn't belong to me (and I know the student also felt like it didn't belong to him either). Kellan did look kind of silly for not following the proper hierarchy to complain, and all those e-mails only took him right back to the first line of action: myself and my division chair.

Qualifier on this: If your problem with the prof is so serious that you feel you need further back-up, see Chapter 31.

Ask Yourself This:

Is my issue something that should be solved by e-mail? Will I get a faster resolution if I see my prof or call her on the phone? Can I keep my anger in check that way? Have I asked someone else to read my e-mail to make sure it doesn't carry an angry or offensive tone that could get me in trouble? Why am I so angry and who am I really mad at?

Think This:

This isn't the first or last time I'm going to feel angry about something or someone in college. Using e-mail to spew isn't worth it. I need to get to the real reason I'm so upset, take responsibility if the problem is about me, or try to figure out my options if the issue belongs to my prof.

Not That:

I'm pissed, and my professor deserves to hear exactly what I have to say!

Your prof may deserve your harsh words, but better words will get your point across—and you'll have a shot at actually resolving the issue.

Say This:

Let's say you're angry over a grade you received. In an e-mail or in person, (preferably in person), say,

Professor, I received my grade on the last assignment and I'm surprised it was lower than I was expecting. I looked at the samples you provided, checked the rubric, and thought I was doing everything correctly. I feel frustrated that I thought I nailed this assignment and did what you said, but the grade I received is less than I was trying for. Can you please explain to me more fully where I went wrong? Can we meet to discuss this?

Not That:

Professor, your grading is totally out of whack. I really worked hard on this assignment and did NOT deserve what you gave me. I don't know if you're tired, or grading too many papers, fighting with your husband, or what, but I am so mad!

You know that my running theme is to always tell the prof what you've already done to solve your own problem. As in the "Say This" example above, the student will explain that he already reviewed certain documents. Also, the student is using continued "I" language, rather than "you." The word *you* has blame, blame, blame all over it. You will get much further owning your feelings—whatever they are—rather than blaming others.

(And saying "*I* think YOU suck!" does not count!).

The End Note

Remember Christiana and her e-mail attack? She finished the term. Her grade wasn't outstanding, but definitely passable. Had she continued her escalating e-mails, she could have gotten herself in serious trouble for misconduct.

If you're pissed off at your professor, go ahead and write the e-mail, if that makes you feel better. But don't send it! Read the e-mail again a few hours later and try to pull out the key issues. Eliminate the emotion and take the list to an appointment with your prof.

It's totally okay for you to be mad, but don't embarrass yourself by sending a permanent record of your fury. Be mad enough that you're motivated to take action and get the problem solved ... assertively, professionally, and confidently.

Chapter 25:

Sloppy, Casual, or Unrelated E-mails

What You Might Do:

Fail to spell-check or grammar-check your e-mails; use too casual a tone in your e-mails; or send your professor crazy chain letters, promotions, or jokes via e-mail.

What Your Professor Thinks:

I notice spelling and grammar in your e-mails, as well as your assignments. I am not your buddy, so please don't start with 'Hey, Ellen'. And, no, I won't share your link with all of my friends just so I can get a free pound of Starbucks coffee.

The Real Story

E-mail #1:

Dear Ms. Breman,

How ya doin? Been having a difficult time w/ my informative speech. Hey, can I get more time please get back to me as soon as possible. Will try to get it done ASAP for u.

I will attached the outline so u can see what I have so far, if u want 2! Be kind LOL!!!!!!!

Thx,

Dallas

E-mail #2:

From: My student, Lina

After scrolling down through 52 levels of e-mail headers, starting from Grandpa Morty, who thought this was hilarious—Instructions about how to give a cat a pill (again).

Lina knows I like cats, so she thought this little joke would just make my day.

The Back Story

I've mentioned before that profs are bogged down with e-mails all day long. However, we aren't so busy that we forget to notice student e-mails peppered with spelling and grammatical errors. Students seem to think e-mail doesn't count when it comes to grammar and spelling. After all, e-mail isn't an assignment, right? Additionally, since students text so much, their text-speak may transfer to what is supposed to be professional e-mail correspondence with a professor. I'm surprised more students don't realize professors notice this kind of—no other way to say it, I'm sorry—*sloppiness.*

Did you know that some profs won't even accept a student's e-mail if it is too full of errors?

That's right. They'll ask you to proof it and resend the message.

If you have that type of professor, he isn't being a jackass. He's doing you a favor. Once again, I'm asking you to get selfish: Do you really want the image that goes along with having an e-mail filled with mistakes and text shortcuts?

Your e-mail presence is something you *should* care about. Misspellings, text-shortcuts, and punctuation errors give others the impression that you're unprofessional, uneducated, or just plain lazy. And those opinions matter if they come from someone who's considering hiring you or needs to interact with you in a professional manner—and that includes your professor.

I've received e-mails so filled with errors that I couldn't understand the core message. Then, the issue takes twice as long to resolve because I have to e-mail the student back saying, "I'm sorry. I can't understand your message. Can you please let me know what you're trying to say?"

Aside from errors, the second worst thing is an e-mail that comes across like I'm the student's buddy. I know the "Yo, Ellen's!" and the "Hey, how you doin's?" are meant to be friendly. Here's a news flash: Your prof is not your buddy, and the tone of your e-mails should *not* be what you'd say to your friend or family member. I can't say it enough: Treat your professors in the same professional way you'd treat a potential boss. And, even if you are total buddies with your boss, there comes a time when you have to get down to business and be a businessperson.

If you wonder if your e-mails are getting a little too friendly, ask someone else to take a look—someone in a professional capacity, if possible. Another clue is if your prof sends back straight-forward e-mails in response to your chatty ones.

Example:
Hi, Professor,

How are you doing? I hope you're having a great weekend. I'm doing well and I saw a great movie the other day. Went with my best friend and we had a great time.

Hey, I have a question for you. Can you tell me when our journal is due?

Thanks,

Anthony

And your professor's response:
Anthony,

November 3rd, midnight.

Thanks,

Professor

Your prof may say, "Glad you're having a good weekend, too" or something vaguely personal. But as I've said before, your prof's main mission is to solve your problem, not to be your friend.

An irritating form of casual e-mails between students and profs comes in the form of e-mail jokes, inspirational stories, or chain e-mails. Many students have no idea that forwarded e-mails have no place in the professor's in-box. A prof probably won't e-mail back and say, "Hey, very funny!" or "Oh, I found that so encouraging!" The prof also won't say, "I *really* wish you wouldn't clutter my e-mail account with this!" He will likely give a small grunt, hit delete, and think you're pretty clueless for sending the e-mail in the first place.

Unless the content is going to make your prof fall from her chair in laughter spasms, e-mails that are promotional, inspirational, or funny in nature are usually just annoying. Plus that, if you're sharing a discount or some sort of offer, there could be an ethical issue if your prof actually accepts what you're sending. If the material is religious or political, your prof may find it highly offensive—even if she has the same beliefs you do. Don't risk crossing a boundary.

Ask Yourself This:

What stops me from editing/reviewing my e-mails before sending them? Am I too rushed? Unsure of proper grammar/punctuation use? Am I willing to improve my e-mail image now and ask someone else to proof an e-mail for me before I send it if I'm unsure? Does my e-mail sound like something I'd send to a friend or family member? Is this e-mail related to my class in any way? Have I considered it may not be appropriate for my professor?

Think This:

I deserve to have my e-mail represent me properly. I want to start corresponding like a professional. I can be friendly without getting too personal or casual. There's no reason to wait because e-mailing with my prof and watching those mistakes is great practice for later. If I wonder about how to properly say something in e-mail, I can ask my professor (or a Business Comm or Business Technology professor) for advice.

I may have something really funny or powerful to share, but my prof doesn't necessarily have to see it. If I think the content relates to my prof or the class in some way, I can let the prof know what I want to send and ask if he minds. That's better than the risk of offending him.

Not That:

Who even uses e-mail anymore? Why does it matter?

Colleges and millions of businesses still use e-mail as their primary source of communication. You may have shifted from e-mail to texting, Twitter, FourSquare, or Facebook in your personal life, but the rest of the professional and academic world is still e-mailing "old school." You'll still be ahead of the game by getting on board and mastering that part of the business world.

Say This:

I'll frame this one a little differently and give you some general things you should say properly in your e-mails:

- Spell the recipient's name correctly. Do extra research to find out the correct spelling *before you send the e-mail!* Your syllabus should tell you how the person wants to be addressed. If in doubt, you can say "Professor Bremen" or "Ellen Bremen."
- You can begin with Dear, which is fine. "Hey" is inappropriate.
- Don't forget the subject line. Spell-check that, too, because it's the first thing your recipient will see.
- Keep the content of your e-mail properly formatted with paragraphs and do your best to achieve perfect punctuation, spelling, and grammar. Copy your message in a Word document and use Word's spelling/grammar tools to check it, if you have to. This extra step is important.
- Close with "Thank you," or "Respectfully," or just sign your name. If you know for certain your prof knows who you are, then you can sign your first name. However, it's better to err on the side of caution with the first e-mail and sign your full name and even the name of the class and time of your class.
- Content of the e-mail is not something I want to skip, but I realize every e-mail will have a different purpose. Just know professional e-mail isn't meant to be a novel or even a short story. In the previous chapter, I discussed the fact that some issues are better handled in person or on the phone. If your e-mail is too long, it may be time to move the communication live.
- Beware revenge of the screaming caps: "I WAS HAVING TROUBLE WITH THE PERSUASIVE OUTLINE. I TRIED TO EMAIL IT, BUT IT WAS UNLOCATED." (Yes, an actual excerpt from an e-mail.). Use capital letters where they belong, and never for an entire sentence.

If you've already sent e-mails with errors and now you see the light, you can always say to your prof, "I sent you e-mails I didn't proof as well as I should have. I'd like to work on sending cleaner e-mails that are more professional. I'm going to work on this, and if you see I'm doing something incorrectly, I'd appreciate you telling me." Most profs will be impressed with you for taking this action, and glad to help you.

An important note, which may be an unpopular recommendation: Be extremely careful about sending e-mails from your phone. If you're answering or asking a quick question and have absolutely no other way to send the e-mail (and you won't be at a laptop or other computer for hours), then go ahead. But make this phone-based e-mail brief because the formatting is likely to be chopped up on the college e-mail. I've had e-mails several paragraphs long that merge into one gigantic unreadable blob on my screen.

Your prof will see the little indicator at the bottom "Sent from my iPhone" or "Typed with my fat fingers" (A real "signature" line ... cute, but not cute enough to make up for a big, messy e-mail) and know you were on the move when you sent it. Not that you can't be on the move, but if your e-mail is something that deserves time to construct, then give yourself that time—on a laptop, desktop, or iPad.

Not That:

> If you don't like my e-mails, then that's really your problem. It's ridiculous to get picky over a few mistakes.

If the prof can't make heads or tails of what you have to say, or refuses to read your error-riddled e-mail, then actually, it *is* your problem. The problem or question that triggered you to e-mail in the first place won't be addressed.

> My professor will like me more or give me a better grade if I lay on the charm.

Honestly, your professor will like you more if you don't. Professors can see through phoniness. Also, your prof doesn't have to like you. "Like" is a bonus in the student-professor relationship. Your prof has to teach you in an effective way and treat you with respect. And vice versa. Do your work, ask questions, and be interested and engaged in class. Your professor will appreciate you more than you'll ever know.

Say This:

I'm going to show you examples of actual student e-mails that are well-done. The content has been tweaked for anonymity:

Example #1:

Dear Ellen, *(which is what I ask my students to call me)*

I hope you had a good weekend. *(It's totally okay to say this, just don't make your prof answer it.)*

I have debated if I was actually going to send these to you so early, but ultimately came to the conclusion that it really can't hurt. :) *(Student shows some personality here without being inappropriate. Quickly gets to the point)*

Please let me know if I need to change anything or if I'm way off base in what you expect from this assignment. *(Assertive statement saying what the student wants me to do.)*

Thanks. *(Fine way to close!)*

First Name *(I know this student well.)*

Example #2:

Dear Ellen Bremen, *(my full name, even though this student and I had plenty of interactions and first name would have been fine.)*

I have attached my current outline. I'm not submitting this at this time for grading (I will send again tonight after a final review), but if you have extra time for a proof read I'd appreciate it. I think it looks good. When I write I have to put it down for a few hours and come back to make things the way I want. *(Again, gets right to the point, and adds a personal note about the process, which is fine.)*

I have a couple questions about format, specifically is a docx acceptable and is this saved properly (#3 on outline evaluation checklist)? *(Good specific questions!)*

You are responding to the class more than any other teacher I have run into and doing so with effective replies, not further confusion. I'm a busy parent, too, and appreciate the time you take for our class. *(Always nice to have a compliment about what you appreciate, but not necessary if you can't say anything sincere).*

Thank you,

First Name

Speaking of promotions or "questionable" emails, before sending, you could ask, "Professor, I saw this coupon for the chocolate you said you like. I thought I'd forward the e-mail to you." Your prof may say, "Oh, I'm on a chocolate fast, but thank you." Don't take offense.

If you want to invite your professor to something, such as a concert or other performance you're involved in, you can either say, "I'm performing in a theater production this weekend, so if you like theater, I'd be glad to send you the information." Or just send the e-mail and say, "I thought I'd let you know that I'm in a play downtown this weekend, if you enjoy going to the theatre. Thanks for reading and no need to respond."

Don't be upset if your prof doesn't bite. Each professor has a different level of comfort for fraternizing (I'd love to find another word, but this one works well) with students outside of college.

If what you have to share is truly relevant to your class, explain what you're sending. Never, ever send just a link, which students often do, unfortunately. Say, "Professor, I saw a video on YouTube that fits what we're talking about this week. Here's the link. I hope you find it as interesting as I did."

Not That:

Here's an e-mail that needed a re-do:

Hey, Ms. B! (*Did I say casual?*)

What's up today? (*Where do I begin? With my child who threw a tantrum because I wouldn't let him watch Thomas the Tank Engine before preschool?*)

i missed the two people i was going to evaluate, is there any way i can make that up? maybe by doing two extra next time? (*Aside from lack of capitalization, college work usually doesn't happen with negotiation.*)

You are my fave! (*Ugh! Remember what I said about sincere?*)

(no signature) (*Ugh, times two!*)

"Oh, wow! My prof just has to read about this! She's been doing such a great job with our class, I really want her to get that free pound of coffee!" Your prof is probably getting these scams (along with fund-raising requests, religious inspirations, and stories) on her own Facebook page and personal e-mail. Remember the fine ethical lines about this sort of thing. Your heart will be in the right place: You may like your prof and want her to benefit from your opportunity, but it's so much better to err on the side of caution.

"Would you please come to my play?" You don't want to make your prof uncomfortable by directly asking him to donate money or attend a play or other event.

"Keep this e-mail going!" This is in reference to chain e-mails, of course, or "Share this e-mail with six of your friends." Remember, your prof can't use her college computer this way, and she certainly isn't going to tick off her colleagues by adding them to the list.

The End Note

You may find a professor who doesn't require you to proof e-mails. He will accept your e-mails with all the mistakes and still get back to you. Does this mean you should let go of that "raise my e-mail image" goal? (Because I know you now have one). No! Take the high road and start your excellence-in-e-mail campaign anyway (this is not a campaign that requires any sort of chain letter! Too bad, right?). Doesn't that sound like an awesome mission?

When others are impressed by your professionalism, and you're seen as someone who deserves a response, you'll be glad you started in college!

Chapter 26

Responding to Your Professor's E-mails

What You Might Do:
Ignore your professor's e-mail.

What Your Professor Thinks:
I've taken the time to e-mail you. Have the courtesy to respond.

The Real Story

Here are some sample e-mails I've sent to students in the past year:

Dear Florine,

In reviewing our class roster, I see you're still enrolled in the course, but I haven't seen you since the third week. I hope you're doing all right and would like to know if you plan to return to class. If this term didn't work out for you, please remember to withdraw the course by the drop date, or I will have no choice but to give you a 0.0. Professor withdrawals are not permitted after the first week.

Once again, I hope you're doing okay. Please contact me if you have any questions.

Ellen

Florine's response: None.

Ready for another?

I'd been working with Brian to get through my Intro to Comm class. Brian wasn't terrified about the speaking part, he was terrified of the writing part (it usually goes the other way). I thought Brian and I worked out all the issues and he was ready to go. However, while I was away at a conference, I looked on my roster and, sure enough, Brian dropped the class.

Dear Brian,

I was sad to see you dropped the class. I suspect you ultimately didn't feel comfortable with the speech, and I sincerely wish you had contacted me again for more help. There were other options we could have considered. Really, you had all the tools to make that speech work. You can do this!

I wish you all the best.

Ellen

Brian's response: Let's just say I'm not holding my breath.

And now for e-mail #3—a common scenario:

Hello, Vincent,

I was trying to open your outline draft, but it's in a format I am unable to read. The deadline to submit for my review is today at 5 p.m. I'd like to take a look at this for you and give you feedback, so would you please e-mail me back and attach a copy in .doc, .docx, or .rtf?

Thanks,

Ellen

Vincent's response:

None at the time, but he had a lot to say when the final outline received a poor grade: "Wait, why didn't you review my outline? I sent it to you!"

Then my response:

"I did receive your outline, but I couldn't open it. I e-mailed you, but didn't hear back. Did you get my e-mail?"

Vincent's response:

None. (I would be dead by now if I *was* holding my breath).

The Back Story

You've heard me say too many times that profs are busy. If we're in a teaching institution, then, certainly our first line of busy involves serving you, the student. Even with that in mind, many profs will never, ever chase you down to find out if you're all right, check to see if you finished work, determine if you're still in the class, etc. Is this because they don't care what's happening to you?

No. Although I guess there may be some out there who don't give a damn—I mean, you find that in every profession, right? But most professors believe that in college it's *your* responsibility to care enough about *your* status in the class, and *your* grades, that you'll tell them what's going on.

If you do get an e-mail like the ones I showed above, I'm not saying you should bow down, roll out a red carpet from your prof's office, and toss rose petals at her feet.

I *am* saying you should at least respond. Your prof is taking an interest in your well-being, your success in school, and your status in her class. Honor the effort and show your appreciation by hitting Reply rather than Delete.

I'm not making light of why students don't respond to professors: Sometimes they feel ashamed or they don't know what to say in return.

I mean, who wants to admit she totally screwed up her work?

Who wants to admit that he's so utterly confused that his head aches?

Who wants to admit her out-of-school life sucks so badly that the stress of school seems impossible to bear?

You know what?

You can be the person courageous enough to own up to where you are, particularly if another person in your world—your professor—sees enough of your big picture and cares enough to help you along.

Ask Yourself This:

Why am I not e-mailing my professor? Am I embarrassed? Scared? Unsure of what to say? What do I think will happen if I tell my prof the truth—whatever the truth is? Do I think the prof will think I'm lazy? Stupid? A bad person? What do I think that the prof will think of me if I don't respond? Is that worse than if I just take responsibility for what's going on?

Think This:

I might as well be honest about why I'm not in class (didn't finish my work, etc.). My prof has seen other students go through many things. My prof may have even gone through stuff himself when he was in college. If my prof is checking in with me via e-mail, I should write back and see what kind of help is available to me. At the very least, I should consider his advice.

Not That:

My prof should just leave me alone. Can't she take a hint that I didn't e-mail back for a reason?

I may sound like a 9-year-old for saying this, but excuse (or, rather, "excuuuuuuse") your prof for caring about you! Like I said, some professors would never try to contact you.

I'm just going to hit Delete, because I don't know what to say.

Anything you end up saying—even if you fumble over your words—is better than no response at all. If you made the decision to stop going to class and your professor e-mails you, then stand tall on your decision and say what you intend to do. I'll explain below that you don't have to tell your story. You just need to respond.

Say This:

Let's focus on what each of the students showcased above could have said in response:

Student who stopped showing up:
Dear Ellen,

I really appreciate you checking in on me. I have missed a lot of class. Some things happened and this turned out not to be the best term for me. I will withdraw the class by the drop date and hopefully see you next term.

Thanks again,
Florine

See? No elaborate explanation required ... just a response! You may not picture yourself ever seeing this professor again, but who knows what the future will bring? The prof went out of his way to check on you and responding is the right thing to do.

Not feeling that nice, you say? Okay... try this:
Ellen,

Thanks for your e-mail. This class was not the right fit for me. I will drop so I won't get a 0.0. I appreciate the reminder.

Florine

Really feeling not nice? Then it's okay to say what you despised about the course, as long as your words are assertive and professional, such as: "I might have a better fit with a different professor," or "I wasn't prepared to take an online course. I found it too confusing and think I'm better off in the classroom," or "I decided to take a different class to fulfill my Humanities requirement."

Now, on to the student who dropped without word:

Ellen,

Thanks for writing to me. I did decide to drop the course. I guess I wasn't ready to tackle this right now. I appreciate all your help.

Brian

And now for the student who sent the incorrect format:

Ellen,

Thanks for alerting me that you couldn't open the file. I have attached the new file in .doc format. Would you confirm that you were able to open it? Or I'd be glad to check back in. I appreciate the second chance to send this and I'll be sure to watch the format next time.

Vincent

In a case like this, your prof is absolutely doing you a favor, so show appreciation. *Many* profs would say, "You sent it in the wrong format? Should have looked up the right way to do it. Sorry, no do-overs!"

Not That:

Guess what? No "Not That" for this section. Because *anything* you say, as long as you are honest, respectful, and you don't spew a bunch of cursing venom, will be better than ignoring the e-mail. Remember, saying nothing sends a message, too—and usually it's the wrong message.

The End Note

When I became a professor I vowed to do what other profs did for me: *See the big picture for students when they can't see it for themselves.* And that's exactly what I'm doing when I e-mail a student wondering what the hell happened to them ... or warning them of the hell that may happen if they don't regroup (or at least respond).

I'm trying to help students help themselves, because regardless of whose responsibility it is to keep track of whom, I won't feel good if I don't at least try to check with a student and help her figure out a solution to whatever the problem is. Not every prof feels this way, but many do.

If you have a prof who falls into that latter category, then care enough about yourself as that person clearly cares about you. And, for goodness sake, go ahead and reply.

Chapter 27

Using Facebook and Twitter

What You Might Do:
    Ask your professor to friend you on Facebook, follow you on Twitter, or connect via LinkedIn.

What Your Professor Thinks:
    I may need to have social media boundaries while you're my student.

The Real Story

Should I get the snap peas? The baby peas? Or the peas and carrots?

This was my major decision point as I stood in the frozen vegetable aisle of the Publix (I used to teach in the South). There, Josh approached me ... tentatively.

"Ms. Bremen?"

"Hi, Josh! I didn't know you worked here."

"Yeah, for about six months now. It's pretty good."

Josh looked down for a second and then said, "Hey, can I ask you a question? I really need some help with my speech topic."

I'm pretty sure I was in that Publix on a Sunday. And, let's not forget ... I was in the frozen peas! (In the frozen peas!)

I realize Josh saw a clear opportunity to get extracurricular assistance, and I guess I should have been flattered that classwork was at the top of his mind. But, there are boundaries between professors and students that should be honored. The grocery store would be one of them.

Let's fast-forward six years: 2007. Facebook was an all-encompassing part of many people's lives … except mine. I was extremely resistant to joining Facebook, primarily because my face is in front of a computer enough with my work. I didn't feel a strong need to virtually connect with others. In fact, just the other morning about 7:15 a.m., I was madly texting with a dear Mom friend of mine. Finally, I picked up the phone and said, "This is ridiculous. We're obviously both up."

Yep. That's how I roll … er … call.

I am a communication prof, after all. The fact that I like voices and facial expressions and body language shouldn't come as a surprise. Then, in April 2011, according to my sister-in-law, "I CAVED"… in to Facebook, that is.

Why did I sign up? Honestly? Because of my Chatty Professor blog and this book.

I knew that in order to reach students, I needed to be where they are. And students are on Facebook. This meant I needed to find my way to Facebook. I created an immediate personal policy to not accept friend requests from students—at least not while they're in my classes. But then a problem surfaced: Until I had a certain number of Likes on my Chatty Professor public page, Facebook required me to link my personal page. Much to my frustration, there was that dreaded crossover between my professional and personal network.

From then on, I kept my Facebook updates sanitized. Of course, it's not as though I was posting anything too questionable, anyway. With a full-time job, authoring a book, a blog, and taking care of a home, husband, and two small kids, who has time? But one night, (about 11:30 p.m.—late for me!), I had Facebook up because I was chatting with a Twitter friend to get his take on something I wanted to include in an upcoming presentation. Suddenly, I see my student, Ranija's IM:

"Hi … Can I ask you a question about my grade on the last paper?"

I was so taken aback that I was absolutely speechless. Or, I guess that would be typeless, because I didn't respond instantly.

I replied, "Let's talk about this in my office tomorrow." Fortunately, Ranija wished me a good night and said she'd see me then. Wow, and I thought Josh in the frozen peas crossed boundaries.

The Back Story

I'll admit it: I'm struggling with social media and the squiggly boundaries between students and professors. And, just for the record, beyond Facebook, I extend this idea to Twitter, LinkedIn, and any other social media outlet you favor.

I completely understand why students wouldn't think twice about contacting a professor on Facebook (or through other social media outlets) regarding class-related issues. Can we focus on the obvious? These sites are *social* media. Social environments, either face- to-face or online, are not the place to discuss *class* business, such as assignments, grades, etc. (I'm going to put a disclaimer here: Profs around the country vary in their opinions about this). Think of Facebook as the frozen veggie aisle at Publix or Safeway (depending on where you live). Or, let's say you see your prof and his family having dinner at The Cheesecake Factory. You might say a quick "hello," but I hope you wouldn't tromp over to their table and insist on talking about your grade.

Our obsession with social media has caused a number of colleges to implement policies regarding professors and their use of Facebook, such as the requirement to have a public page separated from a personal one. Along those same lines, colleges are using public Facebook pages, Twitter accounts, etc. to connect with students because that's where people are—and definitely where students are.

If your professor has a dedicated Twitter account or Facebook page for your class, you can use it for general, class-related communication, but I wouldn't use it for problem-solving, and certainly no personal business. When I say problem-solving, I mean any issue involving your grades, reasons for not attending class, late work, and other personal issues. Really, you don't want to exchange this information on a social media site. Save these discussions for campus e-mail or the e-mail in your course management system (BlackBoard, Moodle, etc). The documentation looks far more professional within that context, and both places are perfectly appropriate for you to send a message saying, "Professor Jones, I'm having a problem and I need to discuss it with you." If you do carry on the conversation via e-mail, you'd want this to be more official than Facebook, anyway. Of course, depending on the severity of the problem, you're better off going to the next level of communication richness (where you can see or hear the nonverbal communication i.e., eye contact, vocal tones, facial expressions, etc.): Pick up the phone or make an in-person appointment.

If, by chance, you and your prof have indeed connected via Facebook or Twitter, and this connection has no relationship to your class, then respect your prof's privacy and be careful about what you message or post to his wall. Your safest bet is hold off on any Facebook activity with your prof until you're no longer in the student-professor relationship.

Twitter is a somewhat different story. There, your prof is likely connected to other professionals in their field, and may tweet and retweet valuable information that could help you learn more about the world of work. Twitter is an incredibly useful tool for up-to-date information in your field and networking with others. You can follow your prof and even ask for recommendations about who else to follow on a professional basis. Once again, after your prof is not your prof, you can respectfully ask for networking opportunities or introductions via Twitter. Do not be offended if your prof does not follow *you* back. She may have a stringent social media policy when it comes to students.

Let's talk LinkedIn for a moment. LinkedIn connects your professional network to someone else's. It may seem like a no-brainer that you'd want to tap into your prof's network, right? And, it's all work-related, which isn't personal, so you figure that should be okay. Reconsider linking in with your prof, just temporarily.

Your prof may be hesitant to bring you into her network until she knows more about how *you* work. Translation: The quality of your work as a student. Waiting until the prof has had some experience with you makes sense, especially if the experience was positive and productive. I'll tell you below how to make that connection.

Ask Yourself This:

Why am I seeking to connect with my professor on Facebook, LinkedIn, and Twitter? What do I hope to gain by this connection? Am I prematurely asking to make a connection with my professor? What do I imagine my professor will think of my request? Do I share extremely personal information on my Facebook page that would make my professor uncomfortable? Have I displayed the kind of work in my prof's class that would make him comfortably (and even proudly!) share his network with me?

Think This:

When it comes to social media, unless my prof has a clear policy about his comfort level connecting to students this way, I'm smart to wait until my grade has been calculated and the term is over before I request to stay in touch. A term isn't that long, and waiting will give me a chance to show my prof I'm someone worth staying in contact with, or sharing other contacts with.

Not That:

I've read a lot of tips on getting on a prof's good side and getting them to notice me. What better way than to follow them on Twitter, friend them on Facebook, and invite them to connect with me on LinkedIn? It's like sitting in the front row, isn't it?

If and when you and your prof connect through social media, you want the reasons to be sincere. I highly doubt any professor will arrive at pivotal grade time and say, "Wow, Mila is my friend on Facebook and she retweets me all the time. I know she really deserves a C, but I'm going to give her a B."

Despite the plentiful advice out there telling students they should work at getting a professor to notice or like them, shift your thinking on this and realize that students *perceive* this is the case, but most profs don't do business this way. You do not need to be your prof's friend in person, on Facebook, or anywhere else, in order to have a good working relationship. (You can even sit anywhere you want in class and show you're an excellent student.) Just have a strong work ethic and do solid work. You and your prof will get along fine ... on and offline.

Say This:

Before you take this advice, check your syllabus or your college handbook for an official policy regarding student-professor social media use. On the syllabus, I imagine this information will be found in the place where we discuss our office hours, location, how to reach us via phone, e-mail, and our e-mail communication policy.

Once you review, if your professor does have a public Facebook page in line with your institution's requirements, then say,

Professor, I see you have a college-related Facebook page. If I need to discuss something about our class, is this an appropriate place to send you a message?

The prof may direct you elsewhere, but at least you'll get the straight scoop about where your communication should happen before you make a social media flub.

If you're requesting to "friend" your professor on Facebook and no particular policy is in place, say,

Professor, I'm on Facebook and wondering if it's all right to connect with you there. Do you have a policy about this?

Personally I have significant issues with students sending a "friend" request without first asking, especially when the student-professor relationship is in place.

If your term has ended and you'd like to stay connected with your prof, say,

> Professor, I really enjoyed this class and I'd like to stay in contact with you. I'm on Facebook and will be joining LinkedIn. Would it be all right if I send you an invitation to connect through one or both of these outlets?

Additional tip here: If your prof does connect with you via LinkedIn, it's appropriate to request an introduction to another one of his contacts. Just give a reason why you are making the request. What it is about the other person's background that you're hoping to tap into?

If a fair amount of time has passed since you've had your professor's class and you want to connect on LinkedIn, don't just send an invite.

This request first calls for an e-mail saying,

> Professor, I had your Intro to Communication class in Fall 2009. I was the student who did a speech on English Ivy (or some other identifying factor). I'm now at the University of Washington (or bring the prof up to speed on whatever you're currently doing), and I am wondering if I can send you an invitation to connect on LinkedIn.

If you are asking to connect on Twitter:

> Professor, I notice you're on Twitter. If you're tweeting about things I could learn about related to your field or our class, I'd love to follow you. I'd also be interested in recommendations for other good accounts to follow.

Not That:

> Can you give me some help with our upcoming class project?

...on a non-college Facebook page. Even on a college-related page, individual help is better served in a private space, such as messaging, e-mail, in the classroom after class, or in the prof's office.

> OMG, you should've seen the size of that margarita I had last night.

...on your wall ... or anywhere else your prof has access to.

> "My Calculus class SUCKS!"

...on your wall your prof has access to, or on Twitter, or anywhere else your professors (or a potential or current boss!) can see.

The End Note

Interestingly, I've known students who have their own professor Facebook policy: *They* won't even consider friending a prof until after a term is over, regardless of their prof's rules or even those of the college.

So what happened to Josh?

I helped him with his speech topic ... in the frozen peas. We couldn't chat long because he was working, after all. So, we met in my office that following Monday.

I teach in a larger city now, so I rarely run into my students. However, the way students "run into me" has changed, too. Next thing I know, I'll be shopping Target.com or Amazon.com and receive an IM, tweet, or LinkedIn invite from a student—the new reality of chatting up student business in the frozen peas.

Chapter 28

Laptop Use in Class

What You Might Do:

Whip out your laptop at the beginning of class so you can take notes, but then pop in and out of Facebook while class progresses.

What Your Professor Thinks:

I sure hope you're taking notes and not posting to your Facebook wall during class. Others can see what you're doing and they may find it distracting.

The Real Story

"Aaron Beagleman really loves your class," a colleague told me during a brief coffee/catch-up.

"Oh, he told you?" I said.

My colleague shook his head. "No, he posted it on his Facebook page ... at 6:30 last night."

I'm sure I gave him a sideways look. "Wait a minute. Our class is from 5:30 – 9:30."

My colleague smiled, "Did you have a break at 6:30?"

Now I shook my head. "No, that would be an hour into class! Our break isn't until at least 7 or 7:30."

My colleague chuckled. "Guess we know what he was doing in *your* class. He used his laptop all the time in my class. Now we know why."

Let's take this conversation in a different direction: Jackston always opened his laptop from the moment class began until the second it ended. One day during class, I unintentionally (really ... I wasn't planning to do it) walked behind him and my eyes darted to his screen. I saw he was jotting notes from our class discussion. In another window, he had that night's PowerPoint open (I post it in advance on our course management system).

When we needed to do some quick research to build a sample speech, I jumped on the class desktop for a Google search. I knew exactly who to ask to do an additional search so we could save some time and maximize our resources. Jackston was on it!

The Back Story

On Twitter, a couple of students (not my own, but students who follow my blog) once asked me what I think about laptops in the classroom. From what I understand, some profs don't allow them. Personally, I don't know how realistic it is in these times to prevent students from bringing laptops into the classroom. I guess some professors believe computers are a distraction. They would be right about my student who was Facebooking during my class.

Some students dislike writing notes, in which case it makes sense to have a laptop or notebook handy. After all, today's college students were raised on computers and keyboards, which feels more comfortable, and quicker, than writing longhand. Having a laptop in front of you, particularly in a class with wireless access, provides many opportunities for efficiency—and also temptations for distraction.

I'm equally guilty at times. Put me in a training seminar, meeting, or conference where I have my laptop open, and I could definitely slip into e-mail or Google something unrelated to the task. When I'm writing for long periods of time, I drift over to Facebook, Twitter, and, if I had it installed on my MacBook—I don't and it's a good thing—Angry Birds. Yes, it's happened. I'm not proud, but I own that I can have a short attention span and I tire easily because I'm used to moving fast.

I know students feel mentally challenged and, at times, downright bored in their classes; some students feel that way all the time. So, fingers on keyboards just innocently tap into something not quite class-related. When this occurs, multiple issues fire at once. First, and most obvious, if you're Googling, Facebooking, tweeting, etc., then classwork is out the window. In some classes, you can fall behind in half a second, and if you're even a little bit confused to begin with, a quick check-out can result in a longer catch-up.

Next, let's say you aren't Facebook or Google-surfing, but instead using your laptop in class to get a head start on homework. Then you'll have more time later for other things. This is okay because at least what you're doing is related *to* the class, right?

Really, doing homework is just slightly better than hanging out on Facebook. Sure, you're getting work done, but at the cost of being present and involved in what's going on in class.

Remember what I said about the risk of falling behind? The illusion of getting ahead can actually put you behind if you miss the present information your prof is discussing. I'm not saying doing a *little* homework in class is never okay. In fact, it may make sense to scratch out work (I'm talking ideas here, not an entire 10-page paper) that's related to a larger project you'll do, and then check what you're doing with your prof. But your first priority should always be engaging in your class.

Before we close this discussion, let's not forget about the people who sit around you. Your laptop use could be distracting to them. Remember when I said college students have little tolerance for class jokers who take time away from the professor's teaching and other students' learning? We can widen that net to distractions in general. Some students don't want to see your Facebook screen or your game of Words with Friends. And you probably don't want others to see you doing that either, do you? To boldly or even secretly take yourself away from class—even if others in your class are doing it —doesn't cast you in the best light.

And let's talk about what your prof thinks about your not-related-to-class laptop use: What would your boss think if she came up behind you and saw you playing a little Gardens of Time or posting a status update? A screen is so much more difficult to hide than if you're doodling on a notebook (of the spiral bound variety).

Ask yourself what *you* think when you see a student or employee not paying attention that way? Don't the words *lazy, bored,* and *doesn't care* come to mind? Even if the person had a complete handle on what's going on, the mental picture can stick.

I'm certainly not trying to dissuade you from bringing a laptop to class. There are so many practical reasons why you should, as long as your prof doesn't have a policy against it. Just be aware of what you're doing—or not doing—on that laptop, and its potential risks.

Ask Yourself This:

Why am I bringing my laptop to class? Am I using it productively for classwork? If not, why am I distracting myself on Facebook or other things when I'm supposed to be listening or participating in class? Do I have a habit of doing this? What are the consequences? Have I missed out on important information because I let myself get distracted?

Think This:

Anything I am tempted to look up in class that isn't class-related can totally wait until class is over. It isn't worth getting lost on what's happening in my class or risking other people thinking I don't care about what I'm doing. In fact, I'll make a deal with myself that if I can use my laptop for classwork and only classwork, later I'll give myself an extra 15 minutes of game time (or Facebook time, or another reward).

Not That:

I'll check Facebook or Twitter for just a second and then get right back to the class.

You and I both know how easy it is to get sucked into social media or even general web surfing. A minute can easily turn into 15, and if no one is paying attention or watching you, you'll find it even easier to keep going and more difficult to stop.

Or,

No one really cares what I'm doing. It's my business.

Yes, you're right. What you do on your laptop is your business, unless your professor has specific classroom conduct rules around laptop use. However, just because what you do on your laptop is freely up to you, courtesy to your professor and those sitting around you—and courtesy to yourself—should be your concern.

Say This:

Before you take this advice, check your prof's policy on student laptop use. You'll find it in the syllabus, but if you don't, say,

Professor, what is your policy on using laptops in class?

If your prof doesn't have a written policy, then she can't suddenly decide to start a no-laptop rule.

Chances are, she'll say,

> I don't have a problem with it, as long as you use it for class work.

If you've already been busted for inappropriate laptop use, the right thing to do is to apologize to your prof or to whomever you distracted.

You can say,

> I'm sorry. I became distracted, myself, and didn't mean to distract anyone else.

If you're talking to your prof, you can say,

> I wasn't trying to be disrespectful. I'll be sure to use my laptop more responsibly.

(Or you can say you won't let it happen again … and don't).

Not That:

> Ooh, check out this website!

You wouldn't believe how many students announce their inappropriate laptop use. Keep your surfing to yourself … or, better yet, stop surfing.

> I wasn't bothering anyone.

How do you know? If the rest of the class was listening and engaged in the class discussion while you were crafting an e-mail to your friend in Peru, then someone may have noticed, believe me. Own up to it and then step away from the laptop—or at least close it.

The End Note

Your laptop shouldn't replace your classmates or your professor. I know sometimes you may want it to, but the computer is there to support your education, not take you away from it.

When you're in class, wait before you crack open your laptop, or at the least, fire it up and close it partway until you absolutely need it. Be intentional about adding to the class discussion, raising your hand, and attentively listening. In fact, you should probably lean your laptop screen at an angle—partly closed—so you don't appear distracted. If you want to look like a responsible, in-class laptop user, refer to class notes you're typing, or your prof's PowerPoint (that's right, if you can access it from a CMS while your prof is lecturing from it—then you can take your own notes on the bottom in the speaker's notes section—very awesome!), or even offer to search something on the Internet your class is working on.

I know how hard it can be to stay away from other business when you're in class. Reward yourself for doing so. Then, you'll be a stronger student, and you'll get even better at Angry Birds because you rewarded your focused classroom behavior with an additional 15 minutes of play.

Section 2

Class Issues Your Professor Won't Discuss (And May Not Want You to Know)

Dear Wonderful Reader,

Hope you're doing well as you're moving through this book! I know it may seem a little strange to place a letter in the middle of a book. This is a great time for both of us to take a pause (maybe grab a mocha) as I explain what you'll find in the chapters ahead.

Looking at the previous 28 chapters from your perspective, you may be thinking, *Wow, students do a whole hell of a lot of things wrong.*

I agree that, yes, students *could* handle the issues I've spoken about far more productively and professionally at times. That's why I wrote this book—to give you words and the background information that will help build your confidence in college. I also want you to reflect and rethink ways you may unknowingly sabotage your education. I hope you've started doing that, and I bet you have!

But I couldn't write a book like this without also addressing the fact that professors **also do things wrong**. And our mistakes can impact you in a big way, leading to frustration and emotional upsets, just like I said in the introduction.

When these situations happen, you may feel powerless, intimidated, and unsure of what to do. After all, the professor seemingly has *all* the authority. He gives the grades. The prof must *always* be right … right?

Wrong.

In the next chapters, I'll cover the most common complaints from students about professors. You'll also hear the back story and learn the words to say when facing these challenging situations. Some of what I say may be surprising to you. I'm going to open the doors of college, the hierarchy within a college, your syllabus, and even your grades in a way that you might not expect, but in a way that I believe that all students have the right to know about.

My hope is that you'll emerge with empowerment, solutions, and encouragement that will shape you for years to come. After all, confronting a professor and having to stand up for yourself over an academic issue may not look that different from confrontations and challenges you'll face with a supervisor in the workplace.

You might as well learn how to assert yourself the right way, right now.

I know that you can!

Read on!

Ellen

Chapter 29

Receiving Timely Feedback that Makes Sense

What You Might Think:

I just received a number on this paper, but I have no idea what I did right or wrong.

Or,

I haven't received my last math exam back and I need to make sure I know what I'm doing before the next test.

What You Have the Right to Say:

What does this number mean?

Or,

When can I expect feedback on my assignments and exams?

The Real Story

"If you're giving a student any less than 100 percent, you'd better give a damned good reason why."

This statement came from my adviser in the one and only "How to Teach" class from my graduate program. Perhaps it was my adviser's low tone, or his direct eye contact as he said the words, but the message stuck. Students deserve feedback—and that feedback better be specific and thorough.

This doesn't always happen, though. Some students receive a number or letter grade on their paper and have no idea what it means. Other students feel their professors give suggestions that don't make sense. Some students perceive comments as harsh or sarcastic, although that probably wasn't the prof's intention. The disconnect between what a prof expects and what a student comprehends can be Grand Canyon-wide.

One last disconnect: The time factor. Students complain all the time that they don't know where their grades stand in their classes. Sure, students usually don't ask about grades early enough or often enough, or they don't check transparent systems, such as a grade book in a course management system.

But professors are to blame, too: Some cause heartache because they fail to give feedback in a reasonable period of time. As you can see, the timeline for feedback and the consistency of feedback can cause a lot of stress for students. Maybe you've already felt it since you've been a student. Maybe it even happened in high school.

The Back Story

Let's take this conversation in two directions: First, you're entitled to feedback on your work. You should never receive a numerical score or letter grade without an explanation of what that letter grade or numerical score means. Why might this happen?

Not a reasonable excuse, but some profs have a high volume of grades to complete and don't feel they can spend more than X-minutes on each assignment. Again, I'm not saying this is good rationale, but profs who feel overwhelmed by grading may cut corners. They figure if students have questions, they'll ask after the grades are received.

If this happens to you, then ask for feedback immediately (Yup, I'm going to tell you how). Request, say, three specific ways your paper, project, homework, or other assignment could be improved and earn a higher grade. There should be no reason your prof won't give you this information, although due to the sheer number of students, she may need to look at your work again as a reminder of what you needed to do differently.

You may wonder why profs don't give *more* feedback if they want students to do better. I wish I had a clear answer for this. Many profs just expect students to listen closely in class and then figure out what's required. They don't believe students need more information than that.

Some students think profs are lazy, and I suppose as with any profession, some probably are. After years of teaching, professors may feel beaten down by students; they think students don't give a damn and just want to be handed a grade. Again, not a good excuse, but some profs become disillusioned and then become lazy.

Fortunately, most profs want you to go as far as they can take you. In fact, they may load you up with feedback. But what happens when you don't understand their comments? This is another problem with feedback ... sometimes, you can't make heads or tails of it.

While it would be nice to have a short story written about what you did well, what you really need is *specific, understandable information about what you needed to do differently.* This feedback will help you determine,

a) how you're meeting the standards of the curriculum (remember those objectives from your syllabus we talked about earlier?); and

b) how the prof grades your work.

Let's focus on how the prof grades your work for a second. I'll use written assignments as an example (essays, research papers, and the like). Content will differ, based on the course you are taking. But let's talk about an aspect of a written paper that all profs look at to some extent. Some profs are heavy-handed on punctuation, spelling, and grammatical errors. One misstep and an otherwise solid paper could drop an entire letter grade. Other profs are more lenient. As long as the errors don't get in the way of your meaning, they may comment, "Give this another pass at proofing next time," but they won't necessarily reduce the score. You need to know what your prof is looking for, what his grading "flavor" is, so to speak, and what standards should have been met.

One way you can have clear and concise information about requirements is to find out what the requirements are *before* your work is actually turned in. A checklist, rubric, examples of high-quality student work, scoring sheet, and similar items can help you to compare what you have done to what's actually required. This way, you can choose how hard you need to work for the grade you want—and the feedback you get hopefully won't be a big surprise. You have the right to ask your professor,

Can you go over how we'll be graded on this assignment?

Then, take good notes on what the prof says.

If you feel the prof is being vague, slow him down and say,

> Could you give an example of what you mean?

We profs teach our information so much that we may not realize when we're being unclear.

Remember, those verbal tips won't replace the actual comments that go along with your grade. If you receive no comments, or notes that don't make sense, then bring that checklist with you to the prof and say,

> I used this to guide me on what this assignment required. I thought I met the requirement to _____. Can you explain further what I needed to do differently?

Or, if your prof says, "This part of your paper needs a stronger transition," you may need to ask what "stronger" really means. Never hesitate to go back and ask for clarification. I can't say it enough: This is your right as a student.

The prof doesn't have to give you correct answers on questions you missed from a fixed-answer test (think math). He may expect you to hunt those down yourself and, really, if you want to have a shot at retaining the material, you should do exactly that. But on more subjective work (think written work that's open-ended), you need to receive concrete tips on how to fix the issues—especially if you'll be graded on a similar assignment again.

Before I seal up this section, let's talk about when you should receive your feedback. Profs don't learn a magical timetable for returning grades. In my post-secondary degree program, I was told student work should be returned in enough time for students to use the feedback and build upon it for future assignments. But what is "enough time," anyway? That definition surely differs from one professor to another.

Regardless, you have the right to know when that will happen. If you don't see a statement about this on the syllabus, then by all means, ask what the typical turnaround pattern is for papers, homework, quizzes, exams, and other assignments. Profs often forget the angst students may suffer as they wait for graded work to be returned. From the moment the work is turned in, some students worry about how well (or not-well) they did.

Profs also fail to consider that sometimes students need grades to make important decisions about staying in the class. I'm not an advocate of dropping classes at all *unless* the student has...

a) talked to the prof and both have collaboratively decided the student should withdraw; or,

b) if the student is so far over her head that passing will be impossible.

But if a student has no idea where he stands in the class because grades haven't been returned, he can't make an informed decision. Then, he may miss the drop date, which could result in a failing grade.

Let's get back to what I was taught about returning graded work: Students typically need graded work in time to build on for another assignment. I've heard students say they received work back so late they barely had a chance to digest the recommendations, ask questions regarding the feedback, and then apply what was learned to the new assignment. Technically, if a prof waits so long to return work that a student can't possibly use the information for the next assignment, then the student should ask for an extension. (Of course, I'll tell you how.)

Most students won't.

Before I close, let me mention two other grade timetable issues: First, if your work came in late to begin with, you can't demand its return—even if a lot of time has passed. I've mentioned before that the prof can't grade late work before on-time work.

Finally, life emergencies happen to professors, just as they happen to you. In such cases, even the best grading intentions can be derailed. Hopefully, the prof will give you an update on when you can expect your work. If too much time passes, follow my recommendations below and ask.

Ask Yourself This:

Has my prof provided any samples, rubrics, checklists, or other information, such as "Here's is what an A-grade assignment would look like?" Have I asked if these items are available? When I receive my grades, do I usually understand why I received a grade? Do I feel scared to ask for specifics? How could I benefit from asking more questions about a professor's feedback?

Does the prof have a policy in the syllabus about when she'll return work? What does it say? Has that amount of time passed since I've received feedback or a grade? Do I need the grade from this assignment to help me with my next assignment? Do I need this grade to make another decision about the class? When does that decision need to be made?

Think This:

If I'm truly unsure about why I received my grade because the feedback was confusing or I didn't get feedback, I need to ask questions and I have the right to find out. Otherwise, I may risk not understanding what my professor is really looking for. Then, my other grades could suffer.

And...

Even if the prof will take two weeks to grade my work, I should have an idea when it's due back. I have the right to ask if the syllabus or other documents don't tell me.

Not That:

The prof gave me a 75. I guess I'll just try to do better next time.

Or,

I only care about the number. I don't need to read any of the prof's opinions.

First of all, without knowing what that 75 means, you may be sabotaging yourself. Asking may make you feel nervous or like you're being a pest, but playing a guessing game will cost you more time. Remember what I said about being selfish with your time? And, not reading the prof's feedback and making sure you understand what it means may cost you a higher grade.

The prof is probably busy and will be annoyed if I bother her about my grade.

Your professor should never be busy enough to make you wait several weeks to find out where you stand. If you annoy your prof for asking, that's probably because she's annoyed with herself for letting the work sit.

Say This:

Before taking this advice, find examples, checklists, rubrics, and other items describing what your prof expects from you.

If something in those documents doesn't make sense, say,

Professor, I really appreciated all of the information you have available to show us what's required for this assignment. I want to do well, but I'm confused on line 10 in the rubric. Can you explain what _____ means a little further and maybe give me an example?

If the documents I mentioned don't exist, say,

> I'd really like to know how we'll be graded on this assignment so I can do my best on the paper. Do you have any examples or other information that would help?

If your prof gives you a verbal list of things you should do, you could offer to create a checklist for her. I bet she'd add to it and appreciate your initiative.

If you received your assignment with only a number or letter grade and no feedback, say,

> I noticed I only had a number/letter grade on my assignment, but I'd like to have specific information on what I could have done differently or how I can improve my next assignment. Can you give me three tips?

If you received your graded assignment along with a rubric or scoring sheet and only a number or statement was circled, but you aren't clear what it means, say,

> I appreciated that you gave me the scoring sheet along with my assignment. I thought I did _____ the right way. I guess I didn't understand it as well as I thought. Can we discuss it further so I get it right next time?

If you received your graded assignment with feedback, but had trouble understanding what the feedback meant, say,

> Professor, I appreciated that you listed things I can do better and I'd like to work on those for the next assignment. I see you wrote _____ here, but I'm not clear on what that means. Can you give me an example?

In the above situation, you can also use a technique called paraphrasing, which means repeating what the prof said in your own words:

> The comments stated that I need to work on citing my citations more clearly. I think you're saying I should incorporate them in a way that helps the reader know what source they're coming from. Am I reading your suggestion the right way?

Disclaimer #1: If you get no feedback and your prof isn't helping you, you could visit another prof in the department. Sometimes colleagues use similar assignments or exams.

Of Course, You Wouldn't Say:

Professor Jones isn't helping me at all!

Instead, Say:

I received this grade and I feel I need another perspective on what I should do differently. I realize I'm not your student, but you teach this same course. Could you give me your interpretation?

You don't have to worry about the prof tattling on you. Usually, professor will help each other's students if they can.

Disclaimer #2: If you can't get anywhere with your prof or anyone else in the department, and you don't know why your grades are what they are, then your next step is to visit the department/division chair (See Chapter 31). Remember to bring any documents that will help show your situation. The department/division chair will ask for them.

Now, regarding turnaround time, once again, before taking my advice, look at your syllabus, assignment sheet, or any other document in your course management system that might contain a Grade Response policy. If you don't see anything regarding grade turnaround, say,

When should we anticipate receiving our grades?

You can also say,

Would you mind e-mailing the class and giving us a status update on grading?

No promise the prof will do this, but you can ask.

If you notice your deadline for the next assignment is close, and you need your graded work to guide you, say,

I was checking the schedule and noticed our next assignment is due in a week. Do you think we'll have feedback on this assignment in time to take your important suggestions and use them for next time?

If your prof is more than 48-hours past his designated deadline, say,

I don't mean to bother you about this, but the syllabus states that we should receive our grades back in a week's time. I didn't receive my grade, so I'm getting a bit concerned. I want to do well on my next assignment and I'm anxious to see how I did on this one. Would you please give us an update for when we can expect our assignments back?

Once the professor responds to this, make sure you say "thank you" out of courtesy.

If the prof is significantly late in returning your work and you have another assignment hinging on the ungraded one, say,

> Professor, I noticed we have another assignment due in a week and I'm concerned because we haven't received grades on the current assignment yet. I'm wondering if we can discuss this in class and possibly look at changing the due date for the next assignment.

Disclaimer: If you receive no graded work and more assignments are due, this is not acceptable. You will have no choice but to go to the department/division chair. Once again, have a copy of the prof's grade response policy in hand.

Not That:

> Why did I get *this* grade?

So many students focus on the number/letter grade and then spout off an angry comment or e-mail. Be professional, rather than oppositional.

> Where is my grade?

Even if your prof is terribly late getting your work back, being demanding won't make him move any faster. You have a right to be frustrated and angry, but being assertive and direct will get your point across in a much more effective way (even though it feels better to "let some mad out"—I totally get that).

The End Note

I want you to feel empowered and encouraged to ask when you should expect grades. I know you may feel intimidated or worried about making this request.

Remember: *It is part of the prof's basic job description to grade your work and return it to you.* As long as you aren't being pesky before the prof's designated timeframe, you deserve to know what's going on with your grade!

I have to tell you one flip side of this discussion: I've heard many colleagues say, "I wrote pages of feedback and the students didn't even change anything. All they really care about is the grade, anyway!" I've experienced the same thing, particularly with students' review work: I take time writing comments that will hopefully make a student's paper or outline better, and then the final submission looks exactly like the review copy. But as we learned in grade school, two wrongs don't make a right.

In case your professor has given up on offering clear feedback because he thinks no one cares, I'm going to offer you a challenge that will benefit you far beyond your class: I want you to show each of your professors that you care about getting feedback—and that you will actually take the advice and use it. So ask, then implement what you are told.

During the years to come you'll receive many evaluations and performance reviews. Looking into a future filled with judgment may seem scary right now, but I promise you that getting, accepting, and using feedback is your key to getting and keeping jobs, and also to moving up in those jobs.

Become good at asking for feedback and showing you want concrete and honest evaluations in college. Then, when you're on the job and facing performance evaluation time, you'll be ready with questions to clarify the feedback, and you'll be ready to act on the tips to make yourself even more excellent.

Chapter 30

Challenging a Professor

What You Might Think:

I hear my dad talk about history all the time. I'm pretty sure the dates of that war are incorrect.

What You Have the Right to Say:

Can we double-check this? I learned that information a little differently.

The Real Story

In my Interpersonal class, we talk a lot about relationship issues, as you've probably figured out. One day, the students and I were discussing marriage, based on our chapter about the dynamics of interpersonal relationships. Students always find this topic intriguing—who wouldn't, right? Our focus on this day was Knapp's Stages of Relationship Development, the challenging stages, such as differentiation, stagnation, and avoidance. I shared that I had been married once at age 20, and my father died unexpectedly three months later. After that happened, I didn't stay married for long.

Currently, I've been married for 16 years (so don't feel too badly for me!). I am candid in my classes without being uncomfortably personal, so I was fine with sharing that I, too, have had moments of Knapp's "downward" stages. I always differentiate when what I'm saying is "an

Ellen-ism" (meaning my opinion based on my experiences), or if my discussion is theoretical or factual. In this case, I qualified that my opinions were my own.

What were those opinions? That I believe people in general are not adequately prepared for what marriage truly entails; that we rarely sit down prior to marriage and ask our partner's what a "spouse" looks like, what that person does, and how that person behaves. In this morning class, I had an amazing non-traditional student who was in his mid-50s. As the younger members of the class shared their favorable and unfavorable perceptions about marriage, Ron piped up and said (in a friendly way), "You know, we're painting marriage in such a negative light. I'm in my second marriage and I love being with my wife. Being with her energizes me and she's the first person I want to talk to when we're apart."

In that moment, I'm sure anyone in the class who ever had even the smallest disagreement with a significant other felt a stab of "Wow, I hope I have that" or "Why can't *I* have that?"

I had no problem with Ron expressing his thoughts, even though they seemed counter to the discussion I started and that the class was continuing.

The Back Story

I don't think I'm going to spin your head around when I say that professors do not know everything. What we teach comes from many different sources:

- Our studies and research in school for Bachelor's, Master's, or Ph.D. programs
- What we learn from our mentors in college and the real world
- Experts in our field through academic and professional organizations
- Others who teach in our field
- Textbooks, professor's manuals, etc.
- Popular culture/current events
- Current research
- Our own experiences

That's just some of the ways we find material, but you get the picture.

So, your profs construct what you learn from multiple sources. Sure, we have to abide by the objectives I discussed earlier. We have required guidelines for what we must teach you, based on the objectives and likely agreed upon by a department. But aside from that, if you think about it, *how* we go about teaching what we teach is typically decided by and chosen by, well, us ... or, your professor, that is.

Outside of hard facts, the information you're learning is bound to contain professor interpretation and opinion. On that same note, as a student, you intake what you're learning and then process it through your own base of knowledge and experience. And, you form your own opinions. The difference is that you aren't standing in front of a room full of people discussing those opinions day after day.

Regardless, your professor is not always right about facts, opinions, or interpretations.

Therefore, you have a right to respectfully disagree and tell us when you feel we're wrong. You may not have been encouraged to disagree with your teachers up to this point in your educational career. After all, elementary school and high school have different power structures. But I've said before in this book, and I'll say it again: In college, you are an adult and your professor is an adult.

I like to think that when rational adults disagree, they may think each other's opinions are total bunk, but they hear each other out and, if necessary, agree to disagree or find a space of compromise. If you disagree with something your professor says, the same rules should apply. Acknowledge your professor's point ... calmly. Assertively make your point, back yourself up with whatever facts or reasonable opinion you can, and then listen.

Hopefully, your prof won't meet you with sourness because you're presenting a challenge. It can happen, though. Some profs just don't want to be disputed for anything and you can probably guess the reasons why: Ego, embarrassment, power, authority, and a general personality trait of never wanting to be wrong. For the other profs who are fine with a little student disagreement, you may inspire intriguing back-and-forth discussions in your class, which is actually a professor's dream. You may also help give your fellow students the correct facts.

Ask Yourself This:

Do I think it's wrong to correct or challenge a prof? What has led me to believe I shouldn't, even if I have a differing opinion or know something's incorrect? Have I ever challenged a teacher in high school? What happened? Were there negative consequences? Do I have a general fear about saying what I think in front of adults? Why do I feel this way?

Think This:

As long as I'm not nasty, I have the right to speak up if something that my professor is saying doesn't sound correct to me.

Not That:

I don't have a right to speak my mind, even if I'm 99.9 percent sure I'm right.

College is a safe place to speak your point of view. What's the worst that will happen? Your professor won't bite your leg, and can't give you a bad grade because he doesn't like what you have to say. You may get into a heated debate, but then you'll have more practice with appropriate conflict management—a confidence-booster and important experience for you.

Say This:

The paraphrasing technique I mentioned in the previous chapter can be *so helpful* in a disagreement.

Caution: *How* you say what you're saying (your tone, volume, angry face, folded arms, etc.) can impact your listener up to 90 percent (or even more!) than what you're actually saying, so watch the nonverbal parts of your communication as you say,

Professor, I think you're saying that _____
(Repeat what you recall the professor said in your own words). I seem to remember the information as _____.

Or,

I appreciate what you're saying about _____. I have a different thought I'd like to share.

Disclaimer: Choose which battles belong *in* the classroom and which ones do not. If you disagree with something personal, like a grade or a comment on your paper, that information should not be shared publicly. Contact your prof after class, in private, or in his office.

Not That:

You're wrong!

Whenever your start-up involves the word "you," there's typically no good place the conversation can go (unless you're saying, "You are so wonderful!", but even then, your communication partner will think, "Wait … what's coming next?" when he hears the "you").

That's just not right!

Again, even though you aren't saying "you" here, words can sound harsh in their content and the way they are spoken. Use "I" language to say what you're thinking and acknowledge what the prof has already said (remember the paraphrasing technique!).

The End Note

Here are a few more tips for encouragement:

First, before challenging your prof (or, really, anyone…), make sure you have your facts straight. You'll probably want to verbally cite where you're getting your information.

Next, if you sense the conversation is becoming heated or uncomfortable, stay calm. The first person that raises her voice typically looks more out of control than the relaxed person who continues to assert his point of view … calmly.

Finally, if you find yourself at a deadlock and you and your prof cannot agree on the subject in dispute, then you can either…

a) agree to disagree (you don't have to back down); or

b) request a follow up to discuss the topic again, if it needs a Part Two.

Bottom line? Don't silence yourself because you think you shouldn't speak out or because you're afraid to dispute someone in authority.

You are supposed to learn from your professor.

Sometimes, your professor may need to learn from you.

Chapter 31

Going Higher

What You Might Think:

I'm in constant disagreement with this professor and I don't know what to do.

What You Have the Right to Say:

I'd like to speak with the department/division chair. I feel I need an outside perspective on this situation.

The Real Story

I settled my rotund body onto my couch and put my feet up. I was days away from delivering my youngest son (who, as of this writing, is four) and so, soooooo ready to go on my maternity leave. Just then, my cell phone rang. It was my division chair.

"A student complained."

I groaned. In all my years of teaching (again, that would be 14), I can literally count on one hand how many official student disputes I've had. I couldn't believe one of them was happening right when I was in my weakest (largest) emotional and physical state.

The accusation? I was apparently unfair because Salena didn't like a grade on her speech. I'll tell you the outcome of this situation toward the end of this chapter.

Here's another concern from a student who asked a question through my Chatty Professor blog:

Dear Professor Bremen:

My classmates and I have had issues with a professor all semester. This professor behaves in an unprofessional manner. The professor speaks about his own inappropriate activities outside of class and issues with other professors and students (anonymously, but enough where we can figure it out). The professor became angry when the class didn't complete a recent assignment. My classmates and I feel as though this behavior is unprofessional and unacceptable.

Should we speak to the department chair about our concern with this professor? Other students have had the same issues. Or should we just let it go? If you do suggest speaking to the department chair, what exactly should we say?

For a host of reasons, students have issues with professors and feel they need a voice on their side. Sometimes extra backup is definitely justified. What a student needs to figure out is…

a) how to recognize those times,

b) who to see, and

c) what to say.

The Back Story

In both of the above situations, the students were within their rights to seek a higher opinion. Let me explain how each of these scenarios would go down. I'll start with Salena, who was angry with me over the speech grade:

Step 1: Salena should first discuss the issue with me. The department/division chair will ask if that conversation happened, and if not, will probably recommend it.

Step 2: If Salena meets with me and feels the problem isn't solved, then she should take all her documentation/proof of the problem (graded speech evaluation, syllabus, copy of the assignment—anything that can support her position) to the department/division chair. The chair will refer to the official documents of the course before making any recommendations. If those materials aren't available, a resolution could be delayed. Salena would then explain the situation, including what she's already done to try and take care of the issue herself.

Quick side-note: Let's say Salena did not come and talk to me and went directly to the chair. The chair might offer a three-way meeting so Salena could air the grievance in front of me. Or, the chair might approach me directly to hear my side. Most chairs do want to give the faculty member a chance to speak before swooping in and solving a problem.

Step 3: The chair will then a) make recommendations to Salena and not involve me; b) set up a meeting between myself and Salena, with the chair acting as facilitator; or, c) discuss the situation with me and then ask me to report to the student.

At this level, the issue would hopefully resolve to the student's satisfaction. In the End Note, I'll discuss what to do if that doesn't happen.

Now let's focus on scenario #2: The letter from the student. Professors behave badly sometimes. It happens and students feel completely powerless. If you find yourself in a similar circumstance and you remain silent, you're learning could be affected by anger, frustration, fear, or general uneasiness about the class. Once again, you have the right to deal with this issue and, actually, it's wrong for you to ignore it. You and your entire class could suffer, and the prof will miss out on getting help.

Once you go to the chair, let's focus on the steps that would happen:

Step 1: You go to the department/division chair. Without knowing the situation up front, she will typically say, "Have you gone to the professor about this?" Based on the student's description of the prof's continued reference to questionable outside activities, I don't blame the student for not wanting to have a one-on-one meeting with the prof. A third party makes total sense with a behavioral rather than procedural problem.

(Side note: Another thing the student should do is ask other classmates to make appointments with the chair. As I said earlier, an argument is much stronger with a number of individual voices).

Step 2: The department/division chair will probably take a sensitive issue directly to the professor, rather than asking you to have the meeting. By some chance, if the chair *does* want you to see the prof, I would say,

> If I am going to meet with Professor Jones and discuss these concerns, I'd prefer to have a third party present.

Step 3: Assuming the chair is going to talk to the prof, you are within your rights to request a follow-up meeting with the chair so the matter doesn't fade away. You won't be able to ask,

> So, what did you say?

...but you should get some assurances of what the next steps are for your class.

I would ask,

> What do you recommend for my follow up with you about this situation?

Step 4: If the chair doesn't respond to your concerns in a way that is satisfactory or comfortable for you (I don't anticipate this happening, but we shouldn't ignore the possibility), you do have other options: You can contact your school's counseling services office and tell them what's going on. They have a responsibility to follow up with the chair or the dean. Or, you may contact the student affairs officer, student services officer, or the academic dean in charge of the department/division chair. Of course, in all of these cases, you will probably be asked if you already went through the proper channels (the department/division chair). Let's hope your situation won't come to that.

You may be concerned that your professor will know you ratted him out. This won't happen. Just as professors are bound to confidentiality with students, everyone on campus follows those same guidelines. Let's not discount that the fear of being "found out" can make you feel a little uncomfortable in your class. Try not to feel bad about standing up for yourself or making a case for a comfortable classroom environment. Again, if your prof has personal problems preventing him from teaching, then college officials need to know and the person needs help. *Your* class, *your* grades, and *your* mental health should not suffer.

Ask Yourself This:

> Do I feel afraid to speak to someone higher up about problems with my professor? Am I afraid I won't be taken seriously? Am I afraid I'll get in trouble? Have I ever had to go higher up at work or in another situation to deal with a problem? Did I follow the right chain of command? Were there any negative consequences? If my situation with my professor is one I haven't been able to resolve myself, or something I don't feel comfortable solving myself, do I believe I deserve to get more help from someone else at the college?

Think This:

If I truly believe I am dealing with an unfair or inappropriate situation, I have every right to seek out assistance other than my professor. As long as I follow the proper hierarchy and have my records straight, I can take my issue to a higher level. If my complaint is legitimate and I have information to back myself up, I will be taken seriously and will hopefully resolve the problem.

Not That:

I won't be taken seriously.

If your prof doesn't take you seriously, you always have another line of defense. And, you can keep going up the ladder, if necessary.

Or,

I'll get in trouble if I go above my professor's head.

Even if you send an e-mail to everyone in the college about your problem (please don't), you won't get in trouble. There's no reason for you to get busted for speaking your mind, as long as you're honest about the situation and have information to back you up. And, for the record, even students who fire off hateful complaints don't typically get in trouble. They may not do their reputations any favors, but they don't get suspended or put on probation unless they breach the college's Student Code of Conduct.

Or,

The problem will go away.

Chances are, the problem will *not* go away, especially if you've seen a pattern in your professor's teaching, grading, or behavior.

Say This:

In the first example, the student could go to the chair and say,

I've met with Professor Bremen and I disagree with the grade she gave me on my speech. She wrote that I did not have strong sources. Two of my evaluators thought that my sources were fine, but Ms. Bremen says she did not hear one of them and one of the others were not credible. I've let Professor Bremen know that I wanted an outside opinion. I'd like your help with clearing this up.

In the second situation, you likely wouldn't go to the professor first, but rather straight to the chair. You would say,

I'm extremely concerned about my experience in Professor Jones' class this semester. I'm not typically a student who complains. I haven't spoken with Professor Jones directly because of the nature of these concerns. I feel if I do need to speak with Professor Jones, I could use advice about how to discuss these issues and I'm hoping you can help me.

Then, be *specific* about your concerns. The chair needs concrete examples in order to help you:

Example:

I have three issues that have become a pattern this semester. First, the professor makes continued references to his/her own inappropriate outside activity, which is uncomfortable. Second, the professor is publicly disclosing issues with other students and professors. While this is meant to be anonymous, we can figure out whom the professor is talking about. Finally, the professor was very angry when our class didn't finish an assignment. I can see why this would be upsetting to the professor, but the way it was communicated seemed extreme.

Disclaimer #1: In the first situation, if the prof can show justification for why the grade was given, the chair will probably not recommend any kind of remedy unless he sees a major discrepancy. In the case from the beginning of this chapter, I was able to show my division chair solid proof of the criteria that led to the student's speech grade. I had her outline with the same questionable sources as a back-up.

Sometimes, a higher college official will come up with a compromise that may work for both yourself and the student. For example, I had a student on academic probation for plagiarism. The Dean of Student Affairs called me and asked if I'd allow the student to redo the assignment. I said no because this was the student's second offense in my class, and he also committed plagiarism in other classes (hello, academic probation!). Failure needed to happen—the student needed to retake the class and would not benefit from Band-Aid-ing the situation.

My point in bringing this up is that although the Dean of Student Affairs was not overriding my decision, that person did think of another option.

Disclaimer #2: In the second situation about the prof's behavior, these issues do not resolve quickly. A professor who has tenure can't be fired without a thorough process. Even adjunct (part-time) faculty can't be hauled out of the classroom, particularly if someone else can't step in to take over. Hopefully the chair can help you get through the class while the fix is underway.

Not That:

> I don't want to deal with that prof. She's already not being fair to me, so I'll get her in trouble and go right to her boss!

Your prof may not be fair, but always take the high road in your words. Stick to facts and try to keep your emotions out of it. Also, sad, but true: It takes a lot to get a prof "in trouble."

Or,

> If you don't take care of this problem, I'm going to go straight to the college president!

I can't tell you how many students become angry with a prof and then knock down the door of every administrator, from the human resources director to the college president. Heck, I bet some students have tried to find their college's board of trustees to launch a complaint. Threats won't go far with a prof or a chair (or anyone!), particularly since the college president is just going to go right back down the ladder to get to the root of the problem. **You will only embarrass yourself by going higher up the chain of command than is appropriate, and your actual problem will have less of a chance for resolution.**

If you do not get resolution with a department/division chair, then your next level up the chain is a dean who oversees your professor's area (academic, professional-technical, transfer, etc.). You can also ask your academic advisor, a counselor in your counseling center, or a student activities officer (an employee of the college) who would be the proper point of contact for your next step.

When administrators receive blanket e-mails with complaints, they do take the complaint seriously, but *they* also don't want to breach the chain of command. So, they will likely go back to whomever *should* have been next in line and say, "Have you heard about this situation?" Then, they may let that person handle the problem, or at least bring them into the loop.

The End Note

Many resources are available for you on campus if you're having problems with a professor, even aside from college officials. If you have a documented disability, the Disability Services office can work directly with the prof. I also can't speak highly enough of college counseling centers, which can help you deal with any academic or non-academic issue that gets in the way of your education. All these services are *free* to you! Use them!

Don't overlook your educational planning centers, and even tutoring centers. Sometimes, students working at the tutoring center know your prof's expectations and can help you better understand why you've gotten certain grades or feedback.

With the exception of an extreme issue (like the second one I noted), always try to resolve the situation with your prof first. If that doesn't work, you can say you're uncomfortable with where things have ended up, and would feel better about bringing in a third party (the chair). Your professor may also suggest that. I have told students, "I think we've reached a point where I'd like to bring my division chair in on this conversation."

Standing up for yourself over a legitimate issue is an important exercise in self-advocacy for you as a student. I know doing so can feel horribly uncomfortable and intimidating. There may be times in your professional future or another type of situation (like a customer service problem) where you'll need to go over someone's head. Hopefully you won't have to practice these skills in college, but if you do, you'll be ready to follow the proper channels and use the right words.

Chapter 32

Professor Evaluations

What You Might Think:

My evaluation isn't going to mean much. This lady has tenure anyway.

What You Have the Right to Say (in writing):

Here is exactly how this class/professor impacted me and my learning.

The Real Story

For this chapter's real story, I'm going to refer to my own college days. As a prof, I'm not in the room when my students do evaluations, so I'll talk about my perception when I was in your position.

When I was a student, evaluations went one of three ways:

They often happened at the end of a class, and students flew through them so we could get out the door quickly. Or, if the professor/class was considered "bad," we'd linger longer, exchange knowing looks and even whispers about what we would say.

Another possibility is that the evaluations happened at the start of class, the prof would leave the room, and then when he returned, there would be a tiny bit of weird silence (which could be tense … or not) until the prof started teaching.

When I filled out the evaluation form, if I liked my professor, I would fill in high bubbles on the ScanTron and maybe a few comments, if I wasn't too tired. If I didn't care for the professor, I would fill in low bubbles and, still only a few comments, depending on how burned out I was from the term.

By that time, I didn't think my words mattered much (You'll read an example in the next chapter where I felt like nothing I said would make a difference), so the evaluation didn't get major attention from me. I actually felt relieved when there was no evaluation so I didn't have to say anything at all—regardless of how I felt about the class.

I know many students feel disinterested in student evaluations, but now that I'm on the other side I see the process differently. I know how important it is for students to have a voice, and for faculty to gauge students' reactions. Now, when I have the chance to evaluate anything—a training class, a restaurant, etc.—I take the opportunity. Happily.

The Back Story

Explaining the faculty evaluation process for all schools is impossible; each institution handles it differently. But I can offer you general insights.

First, if your professor does not have *tenure* (meaning this person has met the college's established requirements for teaching, research, or service and has a guaranteed job, short of sprouting two heads and going alien), but is on tenure-track (on the way to tenure), then your prof's tenure committee (the group of peers/administrators/staff evaluating his performance and making a tenure case—or not—for him) will probably look closely at student evaluations.

Committees vary in how they examine professor performance. Some committees scrutinize every negative comment from student evals; other committees discount the highest and lowest comments and look for patterns from term to term. For instance, if students continually say a prof is late for class or not available during office hours, then the committee would investigate the problem further. Depending on the issue students report, a probationary faculty member (meaning, she doesn't have tenure yet) *could* fail to get tenure based on student evaluations.

If the professor already has tenure, then the prof could choose how often student evaluations occur, or if they ever occur. That's right! At some colleges, professors are not required to do regular student evaluations. You may think, "That's total bunk! At other jobs, you get a performance eval every year ... sometimes more often!"

Yup. This is why some people hate tenure—because professors may get it and are never reviewed again, even when they turn horrible. Don't worry, though, I'll tell you how you can still provide an evaluation even if your prof doesn't offer you one.

Some colleges do require post-tenure review—a process to ensure a prof is still meeting tenure requirements. At some colleges this happens in specific intervals, such as every three or five years. At my college, the post-tenure committee reviews three terms' worth of student evaluations during a post-tenure year.

Let me clarify that outside of a post-tenure period, profs are not required to do student evaluations. Many don't opt out even though they can because they want to hear what students have to say. And, they figure if something needs to change, they want to know about it right away, not years later.

Now let's talk about part-time faculty (adjuncts) or lecturers. Often, these faculty members are only term-to-term or they work on yearly contracts. Once again, evaluations for these non-tenure track faculty differ from institution to institution. Some colleges have rigorous investigations so they can replace profs if performance is low. Other colleges allow non-tenure track faculty to receive yearly evaluations. There may be some institutions that rarely evaluate their non-tenured faculty because they just don't have the mechanisms in place to do so (personnel, processes, etc.—not a good excuse, but just telling you that it could happen).

Do some colleges let poor non-tenure track faculty remain in their positions, even in light of bad evaluations? Unfortunately, yes. Sometimes colleges have no choice but to keep a "less-than" prof in the classroom because:

a) the full-time faculty are already teaching their maximum class load;

b) the discipline might be one that is hard to fill (like a profession where the person could make much more in their industry); or,

c) the non-tenure track faculty teaches at a time others aren't willing to take. Think early mornings or evenings.

I know it's upsetting when poor faculty remain indefinitely at colleges. That's why your evaluation is so important. It's the one way to have your voice heard about your classroom experience and your time with the person leading that classroom.

The way evaluations are distributed also varies from one college to another. In some schools the faculty member isn't present in the classroom while evaluations occur; another person steps in to lead the class through the process. At other colleges, faculty can stay in the room. At my colleges, I couldn't be present during evaluations while in the probationary period, but with tenure I can stay in the classroom—though I don't.

Finally, the content of faculty evaluations totally varies from college to college. Many colleges have standard questions that are agreed-upon by a campus-wide committee. In addition, departments can ask their own questions pertinent to the discipline. At other colleges, evaluations differ in every discipline, while some schools have no variation at all—every student gets the same evaluation.

Where this can become a problem is in classes with different delivery methods, such as online, night classes, hybrid (part-online and part-on campus), etc. For example, if you're taking an online class and the course website has confusing navigation, a standard college-wide evaluation form may not even tackle this question. For this reason, pay close attention to the critical "Other comments" section of any student evaluation. Use it to cover issues that were neglected in the standard evaluation form.

I realize many students are afraid to fill out this "Other" section. They don't want to be found out by their professor for fear of retaliation. At many colleges, your written comments are typed up and given to the professor in a document. In other words, the prof never sees your actual handwriting. In a minute, you'll also see that as a general rule, professors don't even get these evaluations in time to make any adjustments to your grade. Most profs would never think of doing such a thing, by the way.

Ask Yourself This:

Do I believe evaluations of my professors are taken seriously? Do I take the evaluation seriously, or am I so tired by the time it comes around that I just fill in the bubbles? Do I believe something bad will happen if I negatively evaluate my professor? Am I worried that my professor will find out I was the one who wrote the evaluation? Have I asked about the evaluation process at my college so I know the facts?

Think This:

I'm paying (or someone is paying) for a product—my college class. I have a right to say whether or not I felt that class—and particularly the professor—was effective. My student evaluation is my way of doing that. The college needs my feedback about the people who are teaching.

Not That:

My professor will see my evaluation and then give me a bad grade.

This is the biggest fear students have when it comes to evaluating profs. I can't speak for every college, but at most schools evaluations are anonymous, and faculty do *not* see their evaluations until after grades are submitted. You can rest assured colleges would not set up a system where you could be negatively affected by your evaluation. And don't sugar coat your evaluation because you hope to get a good grade. It's not going to happen.

Or,

There's no evaluation, so I won't get to say what I think.

If your professor doesn't present an evaluation, that doesn't mean you can't provide one. I'll explain how to do so in the next section.

Or,

The prof has tenure, so what I say won't matter. He won't ever get fired.

Yes, it takes a lot of ammunition to fire a professor, even for what students consider non-performance. Based on your words, the prof may be required to undergo additional training to become a better educator. So you may make a difference for future students, even if the professor isn't removed from the institution (or put into an institution). Your professor and his superiors should know what you have to say.

Say This:

If you're presented with a student evaluation, respond with honesty, fairness, and specific comments. Say,

I appreciated how quickly Professor Jones responded to e-mail.

Or,

I thought Professor Jones was extremely helpful when the class was confused on Chapter 2 and needed an additional day to work on it.

Focus on your learning *and* how effectively you felt your professor managed your class and taught the subject matter.

If you have constructive criticism, say,

Our class could have used a different type of review for the midterm. Maybe we could have broken out into small groups and quizzed each other.

Always feel free to make suggestions about what you think could improve your professor's teaching. If those ideas are reasonable, many of us will adopt them. In fact, some of the biggest changes in my teaching were taken directly from students who had *amazing* recommendations.

As I've said repeatedly in this book, use "I" language for all your comments. They are your thoughts, so own them.

If you are not offered a student evaluation at the end of the term, you have a couple of options:

To your professor, say,

I'm wondering if we'll have an opportunity to evaluate this class.

If the prof says,

No, I'm not doing evaluations this term,

You can say,

I'd like to give some feedback. I have ideas that might help future students. Should I write that up and e-mail it to you?

If you don't feel comfortable asking the prof about evaluations or even giving your prof the evaluation because you want it to be anonymous or don't want him to know what you say, feel free to ask the department or division chair, or even a building secretary, where to send it. Say,

I'd like to evaluate my class, but the professor isn't doing evaluations this term. Is there a way I can still give feedback? Who should that go to?

An e-mail asking this question will be totally fine. If your suggestion is serious, ask your fellow classmates to also direct an evaluation to the point person.

Of course, when you write your own evaluation, you may want to start with the reason you felt so strongly about submitting one: Say,

I faced a major problem in this class and I feel someone should know.

Or, you could say,

> I thought this class was wonderful for these reasons, and I wanted to share my good experience.

Not That:

> I hated this class and this professor.

Or,

> The professor is mean.

Even if that is true, you *have* to say it more professionally and less vaguely, or else you won't be taken seriously and no one will know *why* you hated the class and your professor.

Instead, Say:

> The professor showed up late for two out of every three classes.

Or,

> The material on the test did not match what we actually learned in class.

Or,

> The professor lectures for hours and doesn't answer student questions.

Or,

> The professor waits too long before returning work.

> Stick to specifics!

Or,

> The professor wears bad clothes.

Just so you know, commenting about your professor's looks has nothing to do with your class and a college administrator can't say, "Hey, dress better!" (Because they'd have to pay us more—just kidding!). The only disclaimer to this is if something about your prof's appearance or hygiene is affecting your *learning*, such as that his cologne is so strong that it triggers your migraines. Then, you could note this in a professional manner:

> I struggled with the professor's heavy cologne this term. For students like myself who get migraines, the smell can be a trigger.

The End Note

Please take student evaluations seriously. I know these evals often come at the end of a term when you're tired and anxious to move on. Get a second wind and fill out the evaluation honestly and thoroughly, using lots of "I" language and specific examples.

Before I close this section, I have to make a quick comment about external evaluation sites like ratemyprofessor.com, which I'll discuss further in Chapter 35. You may choose to write something about your prof there or on a similar site. Just know that the prof may never, ever see your evaluation (which may be your goal. I get it.). This means the people who should know what you have to say—the professor, his division chair, and administrators—won't. So, only post your comments online after you've done a student evaluation for your campus. Again, be specific and clear in your thoughts. The same rules apply online as they do on the official student evaluation. If you don't make sense or you're nasty, you won't be taken seriously, even by other students.

All right ... now for the real close: Student evaluations are another way of expressing yourself in college. During your future career you'll be asked to give constructive feedback to a supervisor or your own employees. The student evaluation is your chance to learn how to say things in a manner that will lead to positive change. That change *can* come from you and your words.

So, say them ... er, write them!

Chapter 33

Teaching Style

What You Might Think:

If I have to sit through one more hour of this guy's monotone voice, I'm going to put a staple through my finger.

What You Have the Right to Say:

I'm struggling with the format of this class.

The Real Story

Professor Tweed (not his real name) wore a heavy sport coat in 115 degree Las Vegas weather. As for the student involved, I'd love to say this is another person's story. Instead, I'm going to out myself.

That's right: The guilty party was me.

Why? Because I let my anger toward a prof who bored me to tears ruin my grade, rather than dealing with my frustration about how miserable I was in his class. I took Environmental Science at my community college during a summer quarter. The class ran on a condensed schedule, three hours per day, twice a week.

Now, if you know Vegas in the summer, a short walk from the parking lot in 110-plus degrees is a total drain. Even though the campus is air-conditioned, you collapse into your seat … just short of dead.

Professor Tweed walks into class on the first day wearing, yes, that sport coat. He told us he'd been teaching at the college for a very long time. After he took quick attendance, out came a legal pad. Then, that man … in that tweed … read from that legal pad … for Three. Solid. Hours.

I like to think I'm a reasonable person and a good student. Oh, did I try hard to listen! I started off on the first and second day taking diligent notes, scratching out everything I could in those three hours.

By day three, I took fewer notes. My pen strayed into drawing flowers and stars on the sides of my notebook paper. By day seven, I made friends with other mind-numb classmates, and we passed a few notes. Behind me, a couple of students played Game Boy. Just to put this in perspective, I was not a fresh-out-of-high-school student. I was known as a non-traditional student, which means I'd been out of high school for a while and was returning to college.

In other words, I knew better than to behave like this. But I couldn't help myself. The class was so painfully unengaging and the material so dry that I simply couldn't focus.

Even worse? The measurement of my knowledge, also known as the way I'd get my grade, all happened through a series of quizzes. There was no other way to "show what I knew"—no writing, no presentations, no research papers. Just quizzes. Those quizzes contained material from the slow, scripted lectures, and some book content.

This professor's teaching style was as old as the one-room schoolhouse. He apparently had no reason to change his method and seemed oblivious to students who were falling out or actively involved in Game Boy. At the very least, I guessed no one had ever challenged this professor to change his teaching style.

I didn't think there was anything I could do other than hope to pass the class. If I failed, I'd have to re-take it, and I felt so sour about Environmental Science, there was no way I could ever go there again. Things weren't looking good for me: My quiz grades were abysmal, but I bargained with myself that if I could achieve a C, I could average it out with an A in another class. And, at least I was getting an Associate of Arts degree that would transfer into my university. When you transfer an Associate's degree, the GPA from that degree isn't factored into your university GPA (Caution: Don't fool yourself! A strong community college or undergraduate GPA is what propels your "competition capital" to get into your university program, so you need to do well overall).

How sad that my expectations were so low because I couldn't involve myself in the material. Even worse, I seethed with anger at the professor during every one of those days that my butt shifted in that seat. Seeing various shades of mad red made listening to Professor Tweed's ramblings off his legal pad impossible. I was furious that I was going to allow my good GPA to suffer. I was dismayed that this person thought talking at glazed-over students is the best way to teach them. I was even disappointed I wouldn't learn about the important topic of Environmental Science.

I'd love to say this was a one-time occurrence. It wasn't. I experienced other painfully boring classes in various phases of my college career:

- An education class that met for six hours, one day per week, in a dark room, only lit by a PowerPoint screen. That professor never had to pee, so we rarely had a break.
- A biology class that was full-on lecture—at least in a lit room— but with intricate PowerPoint's and no time for interaction or questions.
- A math class where the professor mumbled at the white board, hardly making eye contact with the students.

Think these experiences were 30 years ago? Hardly. I finished my undergrad right before the calendar hit the year 2000. So, in reality, not long ago at all.

The Back Story

You've probably experienced some of what I'm talking about. Maybe you had high school classes where 50 minutes of boredom was more exhausting than sprinting five miles on the track. You may recall teachers who droned on in front of a monotonous PowerPoint deck or, worse, lectured from notes for an hour. (Maybe the teacher wore a tweed jacket during a heat wave.)

On the other hand, you've probably had professors or teachers who mesmerized you like a favorite celeb and interacted with students so much that the lesson felt like a conversation that you never wanted to end. Some professors even transfer learning to the students, having them present material to the rest of the class.

I've noted a few times in this book that many professors don't take a lot of courses on how to teach at the post-secondary level. They learn how to teach through one or two courses in a graduate program dedicated to college-level teaching. Others may teach 100 or 200-level classes as part of what's called a graduate assistantship in their Master's or Ph.D programs (graduate assistantships provide tuition, teaching, or research experience, and even small amounts of money called a stipend when a person is working toward an advanced degree). Graduate assistants may have some educator training associated with their own degree program, but ultimately, every college and university differs in how they coach future faculty members to be educators. Sure, you may have a faculty member with a degree in education, along with their degree in their major field of study, but this is not the norm.

So, think about this: If your professor was a mega-star student in his graduate program, but didn't receive training in how to teach the molecular biology he was researching, this person may not know what to do with a bunch of students staring at him in his own classroom. Even worse, your professor may model other professors' styles. Then, you're witnessing years of dull lecture formats or bad PowerPoint presentations in dim rooms, all manifesting in the professor who now rambles endlessly in front of your class.

Training to become an educator is only one part of the equation. The other part is personality. Some professors are straight-forward people, who believe their job is to share information and students are there to swallow it—kind of like a trainer at Sea World who throws fish into seals' mouths. Other profs are more open and take a relational approach with students, believing the classroom is a shared learning community. These professors are like talk show hosts. They're comfortable with— and actually love—having students speak out and speak often.

After being a student and a professor for many years, I know every professor has a unique personality and teaching style. I respect these variations immensely. I realize it isn't a professor's job to entertain, sing, or rap to get students' attention (although some resort to that). It *is* a professor's job to give you the best possible opportunity to engage with the class and the material. If that doesn't happen despite your best efforts, and if you're out of your mind with boredom due to the professor's style of teaching, you do have the right to ask for a change.

Ask Yourself This:

What have I done on other occasions when I've found myself bored to death? Have I been able to pay attention? Or, did I lose the information entirely? What have I done when I've had to sit through church? When my parents lecture me for an hour? When I had to sit through a food safety or other training program at work?

Also Ask Yourself:

Do I typically suffer from a short attention span, or am I usually able to pay attention, but I'm struggling in this particular class? What are one to three things the prof could do differently that might help me pay attention?

Think This:

I have a right to be engaged in my education, though I won't find every professor engaging.

It's true. I'm going to give you some suggestions about what to do in a minute. You can't "out" your professor for lack of personality, though certainly, this is something to discuss on an evaluation (Remember Chapter 32).

And, it's important to look at your own listening habits.

If I habitually suffer from a short attention span, I may be dealing with a listening problem that requires closer examination, rather than something my prof is doing.

You may need to re-evaluate your interest in the topic, ask more questions in class, offer to trade notes with a fellow classmate (which will force you to pay attention), or bargain with yourself that if you can pay attention for the hour, you'll reward yourself with an extra hour of something you enjoy later. If the problem is truly the prof's teaching style, keep reading to learn what to say.

Say This:

Meet with your prof in his office and say,

I'm struggling with the format of this class. I learn best when I'm _____ (doing something, talking about the information, asking questions, etc.). I know you have a lot to share with us. I appreciate how much information you give in your lectures and I want to learn this material. I'm wondering if we can try...

(Pick some options that you are comfortable with):
- allowing some group discussion?
- adding a question-and-answer period after each section?
- asking questions during your lecture? (most profs will take questions during a lecture, but the prof could possibly add questions or quick "are you getting it?" checks into the PowerPoint material)

- submitting anonymous questions before class that you can answer during class?
- doing activities related to the material?
- assigning a section to students and allowing them to present the material?
- or any of your own ideas … think of a teacher whose class you enjoyed and in which you learned a great deal.

Disclaimer: The prof may not be willing to change anything and then you have to figure out what to do next. Talking to the division chair may not do much good in the current term because curing a teaching problem is not a quick fix. In the meantime, how do you survive the class? You can always drop, but that's not ideal, particularly since there are no guarantees about other profs either. Here are a few alternate strategies:

- Record the lectures and listen to them later. Granted, you don't want to suffer through the misery again, but doing so in your happy pajama pants while munching on a snack may be more tolerable.
- Say to the prof, "Can you share your lecture notes or PowerPoint files with us?" Then you can print them out and study them on your own. If these files are available during the lecture, make sideline notes or even try to create fun ways to remember the material, if the prof indicates it will be on an exam. That should keep you awake in class for a little while and give you something to do.
- As I stated before, at the end of the term, be sure to evaluate the professor and offer concrete ideas for improvement. As long as you give specific ideas, spell correctly, and use grammar that makes sense, your message will be taken seriously.

Not That:

This class sucks!

Or,

This prof is just a jerk! She doesn't even care that we're not paying attention!

The worst thing you can do is get angry, turn that anger on yourself, and let it get in the way of your work. Your fury won't hurt the professor.

It only stands to hurt you and your grade. Taking action is the way to combat anger.

The End Note

When you empower yourself to request a style change, you have a chance to...

a) improve your own performance and relationship with the professor and the class material; and,

b) improve the class for future students who will benefit from your ideas.

You may feel scared to ask a professor to change her style, but you're doing this person a favor. You probably aren't the only student who's struggling to stay alert and connect with the material. Often, a small change, such as letting students break out into pairs or even allowing students more time to ask questions, can make a big difference. As long as you're reasonable about your request, you can help the professor become better at the art of teaching.

Chapter 34

Accessing Your Professor In and Out of Class

What You Might Think:

Man, that professor is never in her office during office hours!

Or,

We've been sitting here for 15 minutes and the professor hasn't shown up. There's no sign on the door saying class is cancelled. Do we stay or go?

What You Have the Right to Say:

When are you available to meet with students if you aren't there during your office hours?

And,

Do you have a policy about how long we should wait if you're late to class?

The Real Story

When I think back to my time in college, I spent far too much time pacing hallways and waiting for profs to show up for their office hours. I also spent a lot of time waiting for profs to show up for class. Have you had either of these situations happen?

You look on your syllabus to find out when the prof has office hours. You rush across campus to get there on time. You get held up by a friend who wants to chat for a second, so you arrive five minutes late. Office hours should have already started, but the prof's closed door and dark room tells you no one's home. So, you take a walk down the hall. Maybe you go to the bathroom. You get a drink of water. Surely, when you return, the prof's door will be open and you can take care of business.

But more time passes, and no prof. You ask the building/department secretary if Professor Jones is usually there at that time. The secretary replies, "Yes, she should be here by now."

You feel frustrated because you know you have to get to work and can't wait around forever. Or, you have a time-sensitive problem that can't wait until your next class ... or, your prof's next office hours. The topic is not one you feel comfortable discussing via e-mail. So, you wait. And wait. And wait. Maybe the prof shows. Maybe she doesn't.

Now, another access issue: You've just braved a ton of traffic to get to your early morning class. You're there on time, but no professor. One minute passes. Still no professor. Five minutes pass. The rest of your class filters in. Class should be starting now, but there's no professor to lead it. After about eight minutes, the pre-class chatter dies down and you and your fellow students start looking at each other.

Someone finally says, "Do we have class today?"

Another student says, "Is the prof here?"

A different student goes to check the outside of the door. No sign saying class is cancelled.

So all of you wait. You consider leaving because, after all, if the prof isn't there, why should you be there? But what if the prof shows up? And what if you stay? You have a dozen other things you *could* be doing if class is cancelled. Isn't your time worth something, too? As you weigh your decision and the class makes a collective pact to leave in another five minutes, your professor rushes in, hair flying all over the place, papers clutched in his hand.

He has to fire up the class computer, which takes a few minutes. He shuffles through his papers to ready his materials for the day's lesson. By the time you finally start, 20 minutes have passed. Did I mention the class is a little more than an hour?

Did I mention this isn't the first time your professor has arrived late?

The Back Story

I'll start with a single fact: One of your basic rights as a student is the right to access your professors. Office hours are part of that access, and the requirements vary from institution to institution. Whoever is teaching you, whether it is a full professor, adjunct professor, lecturer, graduate assistant, or robot (could happen, right?), is almost certainly contractually bound to hold *some* office hours every week.

Yes, sometimes profs are taken away from scheduled office hours due to meetings or other on-campus obligations. However, if we miss office hours, a note should be hanging on the door saying why we aren't there and when we'll return. If the prof uses a course management system, sometimes he e-mails students to let them know office hours are canceled. For that reason (and so many more), checking your e-mail frequently is a great habit.

My college requires five office hours per week from professors. Other colleges insist on twice that number. A professor usually has flexibility to select when their office hours occur and, ideally those times also work for students. Many profs put in "unofficial hours" because their office serves as a basecamp to do other college-related work. I've seen my colleagues in their offices late at night, on weekends, and some on duty in their "e-mail office" seemingly 24-7.

I realize the email availability doesn't help a student who shows up at a prof's door, only to find the instructor is MIA. But recognize that the term "office hours" can mean virtual, too. One of my colleagues even holds office hours some Sundays on Elluminate. Still, many colleges require a live, in-person presence at least a few hours per week on campus.

If your prof is never there, find out what's required. Any department/building secretary can tell you. Most profs will see students outside of their office hours, by appointment, and some by drop-in, if they aren't tied up with other duties. Some profs are even using programs, such as YouCanBook.Me to make scheduling faster and easier. My colleague, psychology prof Sue Frantz, writes in her Technology for Educators blog (http://www.suefrantz.com—has great tech tips for everyone!) that this program allows faculty to establish available meeting times that students can remotely self-select. Sue says that both sides can even cancel appointments this way. Several faculty on my campus are loving this tool, so possibly mention it to your profs as an option.

Let's talk a little more about the scheduled meeting with your prof, if you go that route. When a professor schedules a meeting with you outside of her office hours, she has probably already worked around possible conflicts. If she knows your time is limited and you've set an appointment to meet, she may have walked out of a meeting or rushed across campus to see you. That's fine, as long as you show up.

Just as you deserve a professor who's available for you, your prof expects you to keep your appointments, too. Beware of committing the dreaded no-show. If you set an appointment with the prof, especially at an unconventional time, such as early morning, later afternoon, or evening, then that person may have jumped through hoops to meet with you. All the more reason you should honor that appointment. (And, for the record, the prof should do the same).

When you set an appointment with your prof, *be 95 percent sure you can make it.* It's also good to be open about constraints you might be facing, such as childcare, your job, or potential traffic if you're driving to the college at a different time than usual.

I also recommend you confirm the scheduled meeting. Sue Frantz has also written about Followup.cc, which will send you an email reminder whenever you want it. She also says, "If you live by text message, try this service: http://www.textmemos.com." You can also e-mail the confirmation. Once you're confirmed, be on time. You never know if your prof has another appointment right after yours.

Of course, your prof should be on time also, or leave word with the department secretary giving you a heads-up if he's running behind. One qualifier to this: If you're meeting right after your prof's class, he may be held up by a student who needs immediate consultation. Give him an extra few minutes.

Let's also talk about you accessing your prof on time in class. Your time is valuable and you deserve to have a class that starts on time. Before I discuss what to do, let me give you a little behind-the-scenes. Tardiness happens to profs for a variety of reasons:

- Your prof may be bad with time. I fall into this category myself sometimes. I try to pack too much into too few minutes, believing I can answer just one more e-mail before I'm in class for a few hours. I usually manage to be on time, though I'd like to arrive five minutes before I actually do.

- Your prof may be delayed by another student. Quite often, students will pop into a prof's office right while he's packing up. Many profs will say, "I am sorry, but I have to get to class." I usually ask if the student wants to walk with me to my class.

- Your prof may not have the patience to stand outside your classroom because the previous prof is always late leaving her class. This happens a lot. One prof slowly exits; one prof anxiously waits to enter, worried about starting class late.

- Your prof may not have an enough time to get from one campus building to another. Sometimes we only have ten minutes between classes, and one lingering student dooms us to a late arrival, unless a helicopter or limo can give us a lift to the other building (and most college budgets don't allow for that).

Although I'm telling you the "why" of professor lateness, the reasons truly don't matter. It's not your problem. You deserve to have maximum class time. Your class should never wonder if the prof will show up at all. Colleges typically have policies that if a prof is late or absent, she must call in so a note can be placed on the door or students can be contacted.

If a professor is habitually late, this is a bigger problem that has to be dealt with early. You can't wait to report your perpetually tardy prof in the student evaluation. By then, it's too late. Think about it: If you have a class that lasts an 1:15 and your class is always starting 10 to 15 minutes late, those lost minutes add up. When one of my classes starts late for some reason, the rhythm is off. I can't stand that feeling. Students sense when the instruction feels hurried or fragmented, or if the prof is out of sorts.

If you find yourself in this situation, you can go to the prof and express your concern that class is always starting late (I'll tell you a tactful way to approach this in a minute). If you feel too uncomfortable with that, then this is a reasonable issue to take to a department or division chair. I'm not saying you should tell on your prof if she's a little late two times in six weeks. But if almost every class session starts later than it should, then a serious problem exists.

Ask Yourself This:

Have I tried to go see my prof during office hours and repeatedly found her not there? Did I ask the department/building secretary when the prof is typically in her office? If I can't meet with the prof during office hours due to my own time constraints, have I attempted to make another plan to meet with her?

And:

Is my class starting late most of the time? Do I have any idea why this is happening? Has my prof discussed it at all with my class? When class starts late, do I feel relieved, anxious, angry, or disrespected? What negative consequences are occurring due to my professor's lateness? Do I feel comfortable talking to my prof about the problem? Am I worried he'll be angry with me or get back at me for mentioning it?

Think This:

My prof's contract with the college requires him to have office hours and be available during that time, most of the time. If my prof won't be there, then my class should know that office hours are cancelled, or when my prof expects to return. If my prof has a meeting schedule that suddenly prevents him from keeping office hours, then he needs to change office hours. If my prof cannot do that, I have a right to another way to contact him, such as e-mail, Skype, or Elluminate.

And,

My time is just as important as my prof's. Just as she doesn't want me to be late on a regular basis, she also needs to respect the time we have in class and not leave us waiting.

Not That:

My prof is probably too busy to see me.

Or,

My prof has too many meetings and just can't be in his office very much.

There's no need to defend your prof's on or off-campus responsibilities, such as that pile of grading, journal article authoring, or lesson planning. Every prof has to juggle these duties, along with serving students.

Or,

I shouldn't really say anything. I just need to sit here and hope the prof shows up.

Again, a few late-starts are one thing; many late starts are a habit your prof needs to change.

Say This:

If you've reviewed your syllabus for your prof's office hours (or asked when they are), and you show up at those times, but your prof is never there, wait until your next class and say,

I've tried to come to your office three times during office hours and seem to be missing you. I need to meet with you. What would be a good time to do that?

You can also visit the department/building secretary and say,

When is Professor Jones usually in her office? I've tried to see her three times now and the office is always dark. Do you recommend another way to get in touch with her?

When you do meet with your prof, if you need to see him again, say,

I'd like to come back. What times are you usually here? I've missed you a couple of times during office hours.

If you habitually cannot get to your prof during office hours, catch her after class and directly say,

I need to set an appointment with you.

If you're the one who scheduled the appointment, find out what to do if you suddenly can't make it. Say,

My schedule is clear, but if something comes up and I can't make this appointment, how should I get in touch with you?

I'm not suggesting you exchange cell phone numbers, but if you and your prof both get e-mail on your phones, that may be a way to confirm the meeting.

If you have to leave work or make alternate arrangements for childcare in order to meet with your prof, say:

I'm going to take off from work an hour early so I can make this appointment

Or,

I have to get a babysitter in order to meet you.

This way, the prof will know she shouldn't let any issues get in the way of meeting *you*.

In your e-mail, phone, or face-to-face confirmation of the appointment, say,

I have an appointment scheduled with you tomorrow at 2:30. Just making sure this still works.

And What if You're the One Who Doesn't Make it?

If a crisis arises, tell the prof the second you know you can't make it, if that's at all feasible,

> I'm so sorry. My mother was rushed to the hospital earlier today and I am unable to keep this appointment. I'll be back in touch.

You can also send an e-mail since that may go to the prof's phone and she won't have to wait to get your voice message. If you do e-mail, back up with a phone call when you can. You may also leave a message with the building/department secretary.

If you simply forgot the appointment, *you don't have to admit you forgot,* but be apologetic:

> I'm sorry I missed my appointment with you. I won't let this happen again.

You may want to just use the prof's office hours next time or make another appointment, but be darned sure you show. Two no-shows would be, well, let's just say very, very bad.

And regarding the lateness issue ... you can tackle this problem before it even becomes one. Ask the prof on the first day or during the first week,

> If we come to class and you aren't here after class starts, do you have a policy on how long we should wait for you?

The prof will know you're serious about class starting on time.

If the lateness has already happened several times and you feel comfortable bringing it up with the prof, say,

> It seems our class has been starting late a lot. We aren't sure if we should stay or leave when this happens. I'm also concerned because we're missing the class time.

You actually don't have to ask for anything after you say this. The message to your professor will be clear.

If you don't feel you can tackle the subject with your prof, then go see her department/division chair or e-mail that person and say,

> I'd rather not be coming to you with this issue, but Professor Jones is late at least once a week and our class is missing a lot of time. We've been staying, but a few times, we wondered if we should leave

because Professor Jones isn't there. Can you help take care of this situation?

The chair will be able to quickly and easily find out if the lateness is a logistical issue, like the classroom transition issue I mentioned earlier, or a problem that requires different action.

Not That:

Why aren't you ever in your office?

I totally understand that repeatedly not finding your prof is frustrating and feels disrespectful. However, if you attack your prof first for what she's doing wrong (even if she deserves it), you'll end up with tension and a delay in getting your problem solved.

Or,

Awesome! Guess we don't have class today!

You may not have class on that particular day, but someone in your class should go to your prof's office and talk to a secretary, colleague, or department chair to find out for sure.

Or,

I'm going to show up late because my prof is always late!

You lose your own argument about your professor's lateness if you're doing the same thing.

The End Note

I didn't discuss the "busy" factor in this section, so I'll close with it...

Often, a student will come during office hours, cautiously tap on my door, peek in and say, "I hope I'm not bothering you. I know you're very busy."

I work at a teaching institution. My main job is teaching. If I'm not physically in class teaching, then my next "busy" priority is assisting students (even though I do have other campus obligations, committee meetings, etc. that could keep me busy). So, yes, although we are all busy (in life, right?), our main priority is to be busy helping you.

And with respect to your prof and the late to class issue, there may be times you're *glad* the prof is late or not there at all. You need a few minutes to finish a text. You need a few minutes to read your textbook before an exam.

At other times you may feel really angry about your prof not being there. Just know your professor is probably not intentionally sitting in her office or car, showing up late to spite your class. Lateness usually involves a larger logistical or personal issue. Sure, sometimes lateness is a power message—those who have to wait have less authority than the person who can make them wait. But for your prof, the potential disciplinary action (yes, continued lateness could be grounds for that) isn't worth those powerful feelings.

Don't be afraid to take your class time back by dealing with the problem if you see a pattern happening. Sometimes, we all need a little help with time management.

(Or a lot.)

Chapter 35

Learning About a Professor Ahead of Time

What You Might Think:

I've heard bad things about Professor Scary. Her scores on ratemyprofessor.com are terrible. I wonder if it's all is true?

What You Have the Right to Say:

Professor Scary, when are you available in your office before our class starts? I'd like to grab a syllabus early and ask you some questions.

The Real Story

Overall quality: 4.8

Helpfulness: 4.8

Clarity: 4.8

Easiness: 3.9

I just went on ratemyprofessor.com and those were my scores from eight respondents, on a scale of 1 to 5. I usually have 25-28 students per class. Multiply that number by six classes (one overload) for the years I was in the semester system (four). Multiply that same number of students by three classes per quarter for my years in quarter system (seven). (Just for the record, I've been tenured or tenure-track for a total of 11 years out of the 14 collective years I've taught). Add those two numbers together. Okay, you don't really have to, but we can agree I've taught a lot of students, right?

There are only *eight* responses on ratemyprofessor.com! That number represents a teeny-tiny number of students I've taught in the course of my career. Would this site be a reliable way to evaluate me? I would say no.

Now are these eight scores consistent with the student evaluations on my campuses? Actually, they are. On average, I'm proud to typically receive the highest and second-to-highest scores possible on our student evals, though sometimes students have had specific comments about things I should change (and I appreciate those, too, even if they are difficult to swallow).

Just for the record, I have no problem with rating a 3.9 on easiness. I don't want to be known as an "easy" professor. Public speaking isn't easy, and neither is clear communication. I'll take my 3.9 out of 5 rating with pride. I want to challenge students!

Back to the issue: A student wouldn't know if the responses on ratemyprofessor.com are consistent with the wider number of student evaluations I've received. Only I would know that. And what if I had terrible scores and comments on ratemyprofessor.com? Would that be accurate? Possibly, but only if a vast majority of my student population responded. On the other hand, what if the comments represented a few pissed off students who hate public speaking, received poor grades, or just didn't like me? How much could you rely on that information to tell you what you need to know about a prof?

(Psst... you'll want to know how to evaluate these types of stats for your own research when you're in college. So, bravo to you for thinking about this early.)

All that said, as a student, you deserve to know what you're getting yourself into with an upcoming class—and the person teaching that class. But I'm going to encourage you to look for that information in the right places.

The Back Story

I have mixed feelings about sites like ratemyprofessor.com and also newer sites, such as knowthyprof.com, which allow profs to post a profile and answer questions about their teaching. On one hand, I get that students may like a non-campus outlet to say what they want about their professors. On the other hand, some students may use the anonymity to say terrible things, and you may never know if what's being said is true. Also, as I said above, even if the statements are absolutely glowing or utterly horrific, they may only be the opinion of a minority.

Sites that let the professor post a profile and answer questions about her teaching have other limitations. First, profs may feel they have to market themselves and put their teaching in the best light. I mean, what prof is going to say, "I'm a total hard-ass and my students almost never get A's." I'm not saying a prof would lie, but we tend to be charitable with ourselves, right?

When I was in graduate school, I purposely picked the biggest hard-ass as my thesis adviser. I selected this person because I knew I would finish with a flawless thesis. I did, and I was the only one in my graduating class who presented at an international conference (Acapulco... woo hoo!).

Now, if someone asked me about this prof, I'd say I had a wonderful experience, even though this person handed me empty pen cases after critiquing (bleeding all over) my work. But these are the exact reasons I feel so positively toward this prof—I *wanted* a hard-ass so I could work harder. But other people thought the prof was a total jerk. So, there you have it: The different ways we view our professors.

If you want to know about a prof ahead of your class—which is your right—do your own gut check!

How? First, think about when you want to meet the prof and what you'll do if you decide the person isn't for you. Investigating a prof calls for time investment. You may have to sleuth when you're mired in classwork for your current term. Waiting can be a risk because registration starts early. And, if you get into your classes and can't stand the prof, you may find yourself without a class to take.

So let's talk about meeting your prof ahead of time, if you're willing and able do it:

1. Go visit the prof during office hours and ask for a syllabus (the current one is fine; you can learn a lot about the flavor of the class from the tone); or,

2. Sit in on a class before you register (another great idea, if your current schedule allows); or,

3. Ask previous students what *they* thought of the prof (the last resort, really, because this is going to be just opinion).

Before I continue, I want to make one thing really clear: *You aren't going to love or like every single prof in college. And you don't have to. You* need to learn from that person and have a decent working relationship. Beyond that, any other good feelings are a bonus. If you only go with profs who you automatically love, or who you perceive as easy, you may be left with few profs from whom to take classes … and you might miss out on valuable learning … even about yourself.

I'm not going to give you tips regarding profs to stay away from, because I believe every professor you encounter, whether she's award-winning or the college's worst, will teach you something. Some lessons may be bigger than the subject of the class, and I perceive lessons that include dealing with others equally important.

Okay! Here are things that you could find out if you want to:

- The prof's flexibility. You can ask if she works with students to alter the schedule if major confusion occurs.

- Overall pace of the class. You can find this out from the schedule of assignments, typically located in the syllabus. Do you have reasonable time between assignments to apply feedback? You may not know this immediately, but you can ask about it.

- The prof's teaching style. You may have to sit in on a class to find out. Is it lecture only, or interactive? Sometimes, as much as you want to avoid profs who only do "boring" (this is subjective, right?) lectures, you may not be able to avoid this. But, you can at least know what you're going to get. Or maybe you want the boring lecture … some students like feeling invisible.

- The prof's receptiveness to questions. Again, you may need to sit in on a class. If you don't see students raising their hands, it may be because the prof has set a tone not to interrupt. However, this doesn't mean that you can't raise your hand once you're in the class or ask the prof to set aside time for Q & A.

- The prof's approachability. The quick visit to the prof's office may give you a sense of this. Hopefully, you'll get a warm, welcoming feeling, but if you don't, the person could be rushed or having an off day. Don't let it be a deterrent to taking the class.

- The prof's availability. The syllabus should tell you about the prof's communication policy, and I'll give you specific questions to ask below.

Here are some professor qualities that are nice to identify beforehand, but you truly won't know until you're in class with him:

- The prof's personality. Profs get knocked a lot for persona. We're expected to be performers more than ever before. Sure, you can get a sense of "warm fuzzy" or "cold prickly" if you meet us in-office or before class, but to know our true personalities, you'll have to be a student *in* the class. And, remember, even a rock-star prof can have an off day or an off-term. I've been there ... I know!

- The prof's interaction requirements for students. Class interaction is not a warning sign! We don't call on students to make them feel uncomfortable; we do it in the desperate hope of engaging students in discussion. Also, we want *every* student to have a voice, rather than those who always speak up. Some profs don't know students' names; it's a bonus if they care enough to know yours and try to get you to talk.

(An added little secret here: There is a lot of buzz about *where* you sit in class. Guess what? It doesn't matter. Profs don't like students who sit in the front more than those who sit in the back. Many of us walk around, which means the front of the room is ever-changing, isn't it? Also, some of my most spirited and outspoken students—I say this in a good way—have taken up residence in the back of the room).

- How clear the prof is. You won't know how comprehensible the prof is until you're in that person's class a time or two (or three or four). This is where you'll need to advocate for yourself, if you get confused. You can ask questions and preface them by saying, "Before you go on, could you please clarify...?" even if it holds up the lecture. Chances are, other students will be glad you did.

- If the prof stays on track. Profs are definitely guilty of this. If it happens once or twice, that's fine, though a little frustrating. A habit is unacceptable. But, again, you won't know until you're in the class for the first week or so.

- Assigns "busywork." Before you make a determination on this one, you have to know if what you're doing really *is* busywork. Many profs assign small assignments to give students practice, and so we can offer feedback before a high-stakes assignment or exam. Something else to think about: How many exams and quizzes are you assigned in your class? Not many? Your prof has to spend your points somewhere. If he isn't going to test or quiz you often, then he needs you to write, speak, analyze, present, or discussion forum post. That's how you'll get your grade.

Ask Yourself This:

Did I learn about my high school teachers ahead of time? How? Were there any opinions that didn't turn out to be true once I was in the class? How much do I feel I need to know about my profs before I take a class with them? What characteristics of a professor are really important to me? How will I feel if I find out information about the prof I don't like? What strategies can I use to get through the class anyway? If I have to withdraw from the class or change my schedule, what backup plan do I have? If I stay with this difficult experience, what can I learn from it?

Think This:

I have the right to learn about my prof ahead of time, but I have to approach this investigation realistically. It would be great for me to find out a little about the class description, what I'll be learning, and what type of assignments to expect. I'll be glad if I think the professor is a nice person or I hear she's good in the classroom. But, even if I think the prof isn't so nice, and I hear other students didn't like her, I know I'll find a way to deal with it. There are many resources on campus to help me in the class if I'm struggling.

Not That:

I've heard terrible things about this prof and I'm going to steer clear.

What if you hear negative things about the next prof, too? Are you going to keep cycling through professors until you find one you hear good things about? What if you can't find students who can tell you if the prof is good or bad? Don't you want to form your own opinions? What if there are no other profs who teach the classes you need? Are you going to change your schedule—or worst, your major—to avoid that person? Of course not! Believe that you can handle any personality type you come into contact with. Because you can!

Say This:

If you want to meet the prof, e-mail and say,

Professor, I'm considering taking your class next term and I wonder if I can stop by and meet you. I'd like to pick up a syllabus. Even one from this term or last would be fine.

(Syllabi don't change all that much and even an older one can give you a sense of the class.) Or, see the prof during office hours and say,

> Hello, I'm Ellen Bremen (your name, of course!), and I'm going to be in your class next term. I wanted to get a head start and learn about the class. Do you have a syllabus I can take a look at?

During this meeting, which *should* occur face-to-face if you have more than a few questions to ask about the class, tell the prof about any concerns you have, such as:

- "I've always had extreme anxiety about public speaking. I'm nervous about taking this class."
- "I have accommodations set up with the disability office. Here is documentation and I'd like to discuss what I'll need."
- "I really struggle with math. Do you have any advice for me on where I can go for additional help? Do you have other resources that might benefit me?"

If you're concerned about the prof's availability and you don't see a communication policy in the syllabus, you can ask:

- "What are your office hours?"
- "Do you respond to e-mails during off hours, like weekends?"
- "What's your policy on reviewing work early?"

Not That: (To another student):
> So, you had Professor Jones last term. How was he?

Or,
> Tell me the truth. Was Professor Jones really hard?

Or,
> Did you feel Professor Jones graded fairly? What grade did you get?

I know I'm being unrealistic to ask you not to talk to other students for their take on profs. We're human and we want to know what we're getting ourselves into. If you're going to talk to a fellow student, put the responses in context: The person is sharing her experience based on *her* individual likes, dislikes, and academic talents. Even if the student says she failed, it doesn't automatically mean that you'll fail. Likewise, if the student had an incredible experience, you may feel differently.

What you should ask is...

What recommendations do you have that might help me in this class?

The End Note

I started this chapter by talking about my scores on ratemyprofessor. com. Although I have an excellent reputation and I'm proud of that, some students don't resonate with me. A few students find me too chatty, they don't like that I don't do straight lecture, they want fewer activities. If a potential student talked to *those* students, as opposed to the hundreds who have loved me over the years, or the minority who were angry about a grade, or who failed the class (again, a minority), then they would get a totally different picture.

The good news about not liking your prof right away is that a term isn't forever—only about 10 to 15 weeks. As I said before, you can learn a great deal about yourself by working with someone who doesn't entirely click with you. This will happen sooner or later with a boss or co-worker, so think of your unlikeable prof as great work experience.

(Hint: You may be asked about difficult people in an interview someday. What a great response you'll have if you can stick with the situation and thrive.).

Chapter 36

Failure of the Entire Class

What You Might Think:

Oh, crap. I failed the mid-term and apparently, so did the whole class.

What You Have the Right to Say:

Can we discuss why the whole class failed?

The Real Story

Maybe it happened in your middle school years.

Maybe it happened during high school.

Or, maybe it happened once you reached college.

Your teacher/professor came into the classroom, frustrated expression painted all over his face. He looked at all of you (glared?), paused for a moment, and said, "Well, looks like this last test didn't go well. The majority of you failed."

There might have been those few moments of silence as everyone digested the news.

The prof was Clearly. Not. Happy.

As a student, you may have felt guilty, wrong, low … maybe, dare I say it … even stupid. I definitely remember this happening to me when I was in school. Most students don't realize that if an entire class fails *anything*—an assignment, an exam, or any other graded/measured product, there is far more to that story than the professor's grumbling and the students' embarrassment ... and their own grumbling.

The Back Story

I knew going into this book that this chapter would be the hardest because the topic is controversial. I'm going to use what I learned in my Post-Secondary Education degree program to support what I'm about to say. It made sense to me back then, and makes even more sense to me now that I've been teaching for a while. However, I realize there will be some opposition to what I'm going to tell you.

I will warn you that the recommendations I'm going to give, if you take them, will test you far beyond that failed exam. Ready? Take a deep breath (I did!). Here goes:

Remember earlier in the book when I got a little academic on you and discussed how your prof comes up with what to teach? I'll recap:

- The college has certain academic standards every prof must meet. Based on those standards, the department builds objectives—what you, the student, should know or be able to do—for you to accomplish by the time that class is done.

- Curriculum that is "well-aligned" (think of a spine, all in perfect formation—we hope) has readings, lectures, assignments, and assessments (exams, tests, etc.) designed to fit the course objectives you see on your syllabus.

- If curriculum is not "well-aligned" (the spine again ... think about a disc out of place), then the content does not entirely match the course objectives.

Let me give you an example: My research area in college was *not* small group communication. I focused on workforce communication, to include interpersonal communication and public speaking. Could I teach small group communication? Sure. And I have.

But in terms of having a strong background in it, other than the content I've constructed to teach my classes, I wouldn't say I'm an expert.

In my college's Intro to Communication course, we cover interpersonal communication, small group communication, and public speaking. It's a theory course, essentially. We have a case study exam that includes questions regarding small group communication and also interpersonal communication. Everyone in the department uses this same test (I'll explain why in a minute).

Let's say that because small group comm isn't my strongest teaching area, I don't pay as much attention to that subject as I would interpersonal comm. However, I have a colleague who's a *total* expert on small group, and possibly doesn't have as strong of a background in interpersonal. So, that colleague is going to lean the teaching toward his strong area, and I would likely lean toward my strengths.

At times, my students have struggled on the small group questions in the case study exam, regardless of how much I went over the material. But let's say I didn't teach it at all, yet the small group component *is* one of the Communication Studies department's Intro to Comm (101) course objectives. This would be an example of what I teach not "aligning" (again, think of that disc out of place) with the objectives.

Of course, students won't do well on an exam if the curriculum doesn't match the objectives, yet your exams cover material related to those objectives. Have you heard any student—maybe even yourself—angrily yell (to himself or others): "That test didn't cover anything that we talked about in class!"?

Well, now you have a little background as to how that can happen: Lack of curriculum alignment.

Or, an out-of-whack spine.

So, let's return to the key issue: The whole class failed. There can be a few reasons why a whole class fails (and by failing, I mean a 60-65 percent or below). I'll discuss my perception of each one:

The entire class didn't study.

Is that possible? I suppose so. But more realistically, each class has high achievers and low achievers. Everyone else falls somewhere in the middle (ever hear about the bell curve?). Now I'm not saying the high achievers are always going to be A students. At times, the curve of the high achievers lands in the B range, which is why profs will sometimes adjust scores and "grade on a curve." The B will become the equivalent of the A on the higher end. Because students usually fall all over the map with their grades, I find it hard to believe every single student just didn't study and as a result, did poorly.

What was taught didn't match what was assigned/assessed.

This is a more probable cause and doesn't always happen because you had a "bad professor." Sometimes, your prof has content he knows is important in the real world, but that content isn't what's required by the department. Then, the prof will try to teach both, but one area may suffer. If the "light" coverage area is content that relates to your test, that's where you run into a problem.

Other times, the prof just may be less skilled in some of that content, as I mentioned before. She doesn't spend as much time teaching it, so the class doesn't spend as much time learning it. Not surprising that a majority of students don't do well.

The test had flaws.

Again, this is a plausible situation. I could write several more chapters, based what I learned in my college Tests and Measurements class from my Post-Secondary Ed degree. It was so incredibly fascinating to find out what makes a "good" and "bad" test question, and that discussion is too long to tackle here.

Regardless, a flawed test is not for a *student* to worry about, even though the issue becomes yours if everyone in the class fails. A problematic test is one the *professor* needs to take a hard look at ... often.

I mentioned earlier in this book that my Communication Studies department examines our departmental exam all the time, which is why every single faculty member, part-time or full-time, is supposed to use it. We have a faculty member in charge of assessment who collects data from as many classes as possible to see how students are doing. The data is literally broken up by question, and our assessment faculty can see what content areas are giving students problems.

As a department, we come together and frequently review those individual problematic areas. In the seven years I've been at my college, I'm proud to say the questions, and even the test itself, have evolved considerably and we are lauded as a campus model. Now, the test questions are more realistic about what we *really* want students to know.

I'd love to say every single faculty member in every single department scrutinizes exams and assignments this way. They do not. And that's why a flawed test can produce lots of F grades. When I was in my Post-Secondary Ed program, my professor and mentor, Dr. McClain, said: *"If the whole class fails, there's usually something wrong with the instrument or something wrong with the instruction."* I'll never forget those words.

In fact, when I find my students didn't do well on a particular assignment or portion of a test (such as those small group questions),

I have to ask myself, "How well did I teach that material? What could I have done differently?" I also ask myself if something was wrong with the test. Then, depending on the issue, I usually make an adjustment on the exam so students don't have to suffer based on my insufficient instruction or a poorly worded question on my instrument (test).

Now I imagine you're thinking about every test or assignment that didn't go well, and you're prepared to blame the prof for her instruction *and* the damned instrument she used to measure your knowledge. Either one has to be the reason you failed, right?

It isn't that simple, and I know students will quickly place blame, rather than look at what they could have done differently.

What I'm saying here only applies if your entire class doesn't do well on an assignment or test. If *you* didn't do well on an assignment or test, that requires different conversations, which hopefully you're primed to have, based on all the words you've learned from this book.

But if a large majority or even your entire class *does* receive low grades on major tests/assignments, you definitely have the right to question the issue with your prof.

As I said at the start of this chapter, tackling this conversation may feel intimidating and even scary. You may think, *What right do I have to question my professor's teaching?*

If your whole class is struggling due to a problem with the *way* you're being taught, you actually do have a right to ask questions. As long as you ask inquisitively, rather than in an accusing way ... with sincerity, not with entitlement, your prof should take your words to heart and investigate the problem.

I cannot promise you that your professor will take any steps to improve the situation. I only hope that your questions will lead to positive changes.

For this issue, I also can't say, "Go report your prof to the division/ department chair if you don't get resolution" because a failed test isn't a concrete problem, like a prof not showing up for office hours or consistently arriving late for class.

Yes, you do have the right to go higher than your prof to figure out what's going on, but the fix may not be quick. For a division or department chair to deal with a faculty member's curricular issue, more complex investigation and untangling needs to happen. After all, we practice academic freedom for a reason.

So, if you don't reach resolution with your prof and you do discuss your concerns with a higher authority, know that future students may benefit—which I get doesn't exactly help your situation. I've said it before and I'll say again: Let's hope your issue doesn't come to that.

Ask Yourself This:

Do I know if my whole class failed an exam or assignment? Am I willing to find out what the class average was on a given exam or assignment? What am I afraid my professor will say if I ask questions? Are my fears realistic? Do I think my prof will fail me just for wanting to know about my test? What are some positive outcomes?

Think This:

I can tactfully ask my professor if she's is willing to discuss a particular assignment or test. I can say I'm interested to find out how the class is doing on a whole (if I don't already know this), and I'm wondering if the professor can look at the test for areas where a lot of students had problems.

Not That:

My professor is going to hate me if I question how he's doing things. He's going to think that I believe he's a bad professor and he'll give me an even worse grade, or he'll take it out on me in some other way.

If you ask about the instruction of your class, and do so in a professional way, your professor hopefully won't take this as a personal attack. It's business. If your professor is well-rooted in his instruction, then he has no reason to become defensive. Sometimes we profs need to look at our curriculum with fresh eyes.

Say This:

Before you have your discussion, it's important to determine what exactly you want from the professor, such as:

- Retaking the exam,
- Grading on a curve,
- Having a discussion with the whole class about areas of confusion,
- Throwing out certain sections of an exam if a certain number of students failed,

- Allowing students to take a different type of exam,
- An additional assignment to help students' comprehension (I'm not going to say extra credit because you know how I feel about that already, right?).

I'm not saying you *should* ask for one of these things, but they're examples of specific requests you may make. If you just tell the prof, "I'm worried that we all failed and you should do something about that," you're being too vague.

Now, what to say:

If you know the entire class didn't do well, make an appointment with your professor and say,

> I'd like to discuss the last exam.

This way, the prof will set aside proper time to meet with you and know what you have to say is important. This is not a discussion I would have during drop-in office hours, unless that's your only time to do it.

Once you're in the prof's office, say,

> I didn't do well on the last exam and I heard you say in class that most of us didn't do well either. I'm wondering if you're willing to take a look at what part of the test everyone struggled with. I'm concerned that somehow we didn't make a connection to what we were learning if all of us did so poorly. Maybe there's a problem with the test, itself? I'm not trying to blame anything or anyone. I would truly like to do better and understand where I'm going wrong. Could you re-look at the test and consider letting us make up some of these points? I am also concerned that if we can't follow this material now, we'll fall behind and struggle with the next test, too.

If you're in the prof's office and you have no idea how the rest of the class did on the exam, you could say,

> Professor, I did poorly on this exam and I'm wondering if you're willing to share what the class average was. I'd like to know if I was the only one struggling. Maybe I missed something important or didn't fully understand the material as well as I thought I did.

The prof may or may not share the class average, but usually, profs will give the class an idea of how grades went on the whole. I consider those discussions extremely important because students deserve to know if their classmates are missing the mark on something, or if everyone else is rocking their work.

If the prof does share the class average and it's less than, say, a 70 percent, you can say,

> I appreciate you sharing that information with me. It seems like
> most of us struggled.

(Then you'd continue with the next part about having trouble with the learning, or your concern over something being wrong with the test).

Now I know I said above you should know what you want from the prof, but first, see what she suggests when you start this conversation. You'll want to gauge her reaction to what you're saying—whether she stays calm or starts to show signs of defensiveness (body language and tone of voice could give you a clue).

Hopefully, the prof will offer something tangible, although you probably won't know about it right in that meeting. She'll have to think about the appropriate way to proceed and then talk to your class. I've even consulted other faculty in my department to brainstorm on an appropriate remedy. Like I said, these situations are not usually a quick-fix.

If the prof asks you for suggestions or says,

> What do you propose?

Then you could say,

> I'm wondering if we could revisit the questions for partial credit.

Or,

> Could we retake a different type of test?

Or even,

> Would you be willing to grade on a curve?"

(Although realize that if everyone failed, there isn't much of a curve to grade on, is there?).

If the prof flat-out seems unwilling to do anything about the exam, then you and your classmates need to make sure this situation doesn't happen again. How? You'll have to slow the prof down in his teaching, ask tons and tons of questions, request any study tools or guides that are available, and even contact another prof in the same department and ask her advice on how your class can improve.

I hate to say this, but you may have to start asking a prof's dreaded question, "Will this be on the test?" You need that information to ensure a concrete study base for next time.

Not That:
You sucked at teaching this information, which is why we all failed.

Even if the prof didn't teach effectively, once again, blame isn't the direction you want. This is going to be a sensitive enough discussion without mixing in anger or nastiness.

The End Note

I'm not asking you to do anything I haven't already done myself. I took an Anthropology class once and did horribly on every single exam. I actually had no idea how the rest of the class was doing. I thought the prof was enjoyable and I knew he was a long-timer at the college. I genuinely liked the class, even though the tests were killing me. The rest of my work was going quite well.

Because I was taking higher-level classes in my Post-Secondary Ed program at the same time I had this 100-level class, I felt I had enough "beginner" knowledge about teaching to ask questions. I was extremely worried because we had one more major exam coming up before the term ended. So I tentatively approached Professor Anthro (not his real name, of course) and said, "I wonder if we can discuss my test grades. I'm not sure how the rest of the class is doing, but my scores have been terrible. If you look at my written work, you'll see that I actually know the material pretty well."

The professor kindly replied, "Things should average out okay for you then."

I shook my head. "We've had all multiple choice tests so far, other than some of the written papers. But the multiple choice tests are weighted high. If you asked me to write a paper about the Yanomamo tribe, I'd do well." Now you'll notice I didn't directly ask about the class average on the tests. I didn't know enough at that point to pose that exact question.

What I do know is that when I walked in on final exam day, to my surprise, there was no multiple choice test. Instead, we watched a film related to anthropology and had to write our interpretation of it ... in class. Clearly, this was going to be a subjectively graded piece, rather than the right-or-wrongness of those typical multiple-choice exams.

Every indication prior to this day pointed to the idea that our final would be exactly like the rest of the tests. When students heard that wasn't the case, you could feel the excitement in the room. I had to wonder if I was the first person to ever challenge Professor Anthro about the way things had been done. Or, maybe I was the first person to ever encourage a re-look at those tests, especially if the scores were low overall.

Because of the change in the final exam, I ended up with a B in that class instead of a C. I hope my other classmates fared as well.

If you're able to encourage (gently nudge?) a professor to reflect on his teaching, even if it changes nothing in your current class, know that you've done the prof a huge favor. You could have a big role in making her even stronger at what she does.

Even if the prof becomes slightly miffed or all-out defensive, *you have the right to question what doesn't seem correct.* Don't silence yourself because you feel like the underdog.

You deserve to respectfully and assertively pursue an issue that concerns you in college.

You deserve the chance to gain confidence; to become a change agent for yourself and others.

You deserve to find the right words to transform the personal and professional you in incredibly positive ways.

And you deserve to take every single one of those skills with you to use for the rest of your life (and you will!).

There is power in your voice.

Go use it.

I can't wait to hear how you do!

The Last Word...

Dear Student,

I know you're probably thinking, "She's writing *another* letter? Didn't she just do that in the middle of the book?" Well, what can I say? I missed you since then.

Seriously, I have two final notes: First, I'm inviting you to write to me. You don't have to be my student to ask a question, get my advice, or just let me know how my advice worked out for you. I'd love to hear any feedback you're willing to share! Just as in your classes, one question can do so much good for others. Here's how to get in touch:

- Follow my Chatty Professor blog, which contains further tips on student-professor communication—http://www.ellenbremen.com
- Follow me on Twitter: @chattyprof, hashtag #STNT (Say This, NOT That)

I also welcome your review of this book on Amazon.com, BN.com, or wherever you order it. Just as I tell my students during evaluation time, "If you love what's happening here, I can keep doing it. If you don't love what's happening here, then I can work to make it better." (Now, when you evaluate this book, you already know to give *specific* feedback, right? Of course, you do!).

Second and last note: When a colleague of mine reviewed this book, *after* she said it should be "required reading for all students and recommended reading for all profs," she noted: "Ellen, some students may read this and still won't change a thing." She's right: There may be *nothing* I can say to convince you to confront a professor ... or not e-mail the college president when you have a problem ... today.

Tomorrow, or someday, you may feel completely different. Maybe, when you're ready, my words will be the change agent for you. I can't wait to hear about it when that time comes.

Meanwhile, bravo to all of you for taking steps to become magnificent, assertive communicators, I wish you great abundance on your educational journey.

Ellen

About the Author

A 14-year classroom veteran, Ellen Bremen is tenured faculty in the Communication Studies department at Highline Community College. Ellen has previously taught at Darton College (a two-year unit of the University of Georgia system), the University of Nevada Las Vegas, and College of Southern Nevada. Ellen holds degrees in Post-Secondary Education and Communication ... and she's an extremely proud A.A. degree holder.

As a professor who stops at nothing to help students strengthen their communication skills: Peanut butter and jelly to illustrate problematic messages, pipe cleaners to teach communication models, and Post-it notes to reduce speaking anxiety, not surprisingly, Ellen has received national recognition for teaching innovation by the Sloan-Consortium (2011), the National Institute for Staff and Organizational Development and the National Council of Instructional Administrators (2003).

She is a sought-after subject matter expert in public speaking and interpersonal communication for nearly every single major academic publisher, including Mc-Graw Hill, Oxford University Press, Cengage, and Pearson.

In 2010-2013, Ellen's work with major publishers did not stop her from spiritedly signing on to the Gates Foundation's Open Course Library Grant (in partnership with the Washington State Board of Community and Technical Colleges) when she was competitively selected to serve on the leadership team. This initiative offers open source 100- and 200-level course materials at a cost of no more than $30 to students, eliminating the need for costly textbooks.

Ellen, whose love of public speaking "borders on the ridiculous," is an award-winning public speaker who, in 2007, became one of only four Washington State certified speakers for Monster.com's "Making High School Count" program. She continues to deliver college presentations through Samara Lectures.

Ellen blogs as The Chatty Professor. She is an insanely active tweeter (@chattyprof).

Ellen lives in Seattle with her husband, Mark, daughter, Brenna, and son, Scott.

Acknowledgments

One person writes a book; a loving village holds the author of that book. Abundant appreciation from my head to my heart.

To **every single student** whose education I've had the privilege to share for a moment, an advising session, or a term, I've learned so much from you about education, about communication, about myself.

To those who have taught me: **Dr. Cliff McClain, Dr. Paul Meacham, Dr. Rosemarie Deering** (UNLV). I live and practice your instruction every day with my own students. **Dr. Thomas Burkholder** at UNLV and **Dr. Beth DeLisle** (formerly at UNLV), who supported my goal to teach at a community college. Hopefully, I've done you proud.

To those who work alongside me in higher education and strengthen me with their excellence—all the faculty, staff, and administrators at **Highline Community College**.

To every single reader from my **Chatty Professor blog**. Our interactions mean the world to me. I can't wait for more conversations.

To my early book endorsers: **Ron Adler, Vicki Davis, Dave Kerpen, Cal Newport, Lynn O'Shaughnessy, Chris Westfall, Jennifer Worick**. You are my credibility totem pole, as I teach my students. I stand so very tall thanks to you.

To two colleagues who became dear friends: **Don Crawley** who said, "Ellen, I think you have something here" and encouraged me to write again for the love of it. I value you, Don. And to **Rob Walsh** because your quiet support always lifted me and I admire *you*.

To my book mentors, **Jennifer Worick** and **Kerry Colburn**. The universe sent you to me. I can't find enough words to express my thanks.

To my agent, **Krista Goering**, and the NorLights Press team, **Sammie Justesen, Dee Justesen**, and **Nadene Carter**. You are putting this book in students' hands and offering them a means to change their lives through the power of communication. Thank you!

To my **Twitter tweeps** who I regularly interact with and who generously share my message. I can't list everyone here, but if you sign up for Twitter, follow me, then follow the people I interact with and communicate with them, too, you will *not* be sorry.

To **Eric Clark, Quincy Tutoring/Eastern Nazarene College** for your friendship and unwavering support. My connection with you is one of my greatest Twitter gifts.

To **Christian Hollingsworth**, for masterfully re-designing my blog and refining my online presence. The universe gave me a social media coach and a new valued, treasured friend.

To **Isa Adney**, for sharing this complex journey with me. You are so heartful. Your light inspires me.

Abundant appreciation from my whole heart...

To **Jessica Gilmore** and **Shannon Proctor**. Oy vey. These two incredible women will be so glad this book is finally out! You are such stabilizing forces for me.

To my wonderful friends in all my spheres who are so supportive. Too many to list by name, but you know who you are.

To **Eli Barlag**, who teaches me about flexibility of body and mind— required for so many things in life.

To my sister-in-law, **Sheryl Prichard**. You motivate and inspire, and your backdrop of support has always wrapped around me. To **Marlene** and **Phil Edelsberg** (my in-laws) and **Ariel** and **Jon Bremen** (my fellow family educators), with love.

To my everyday four, **Jessie, Mary, Jennifer, Janine**. I cannot survive without you in my life! Love all of you!

To my big-eyed babies, **Brenna** and **Scott**. You are 4 and 9 when this book is coming out. You wondered why Mama was always "typing, typing, typing on her laptop." Mama wants you and every other kid to have a confident, competent voice. Someday, you will use these words for yourself, and your Mama will be so proud you did!

To my husband, **Mark**. The definition of true love is supporting your partner to realize yet another dream. I love you for that.

To my mother, **Elaine McDonald**, who always believed in me as a writer, I send you my love.

To my father, **Bernard Levine**, who loved my short stories and loved me, but died when I was 21. I'd give anything to have one day back so you could see everything I've became and the things that have come from me.

Available from NorlightsPress and fine booksellers everywhere

Toll free: 888-558-4354   **Online:** www.norlightspress.com
Shipping Info: Add $2.95 - first item and $1.00 for each additional item

Name_____

Address_____

Daytime Phone_____

E-mail_____

No. Copies	Title	Price (each)	Total Cost

	Subtotal	
	Shipping	
	Total	

Payment by (circle one):
   Check   Visa   Mastercard   Discover   Am Express

Card number_____3 digit code_____

Exp.date_____ Signature_____

Mailing Address:
762 State Road 458
Bedford, IN 47421

Sign up to receive our catalogue at
www.norlightspress.com

CPSIA information can be obtained at www.ICGtesting.com
Printed in the USA
LVOW090300280412

279504LV00001B/2/P